The Pocket Guide to Feminism

T0324361

The Pocket Guide to Feminism

A Survival Kit

Bel Olid

Translated from Catalan
by Laura McGloughlin

polity

Originally published in Catalan as *Feminisme de butxaca* by Angle Editorial © Bel Olid, 2017. Translation rights arranged by Asterisc Agents

This English edition © Polity Press, 2024

The translation of this work has been supported by the Institut Ramon Llull

Polity Press
65 Bridge Street
Cambridge CB2 1UR, UK

Polity Press
111 River Street
Hoboken, NJ 07030, USA

ISBN-13: 978-1-5095-6472-9 (hardback)
ISBN-13: 978-1-5095-6473-6 (paperback)

A catalogue record for this book is available from the British Library.

Library of Congress Control Number: 2024939853

Typeset in 11.5 on 14pt Adobe Garamond
by Cheshire Typesetting Ltd, Cuddington, Cheshire
Printed and bound in Great Britain by CPI Group (UK) Ltd, Croydon

The publisher has used its best endeavours to ensure that the URLs for external websites referred to in this book are correct and active at the time of going to press. However, the publisher has no responsibility for the websites and can make no guarantee that a site will remain live or that the content is or will remain appropriate.

Every effort has been made to trace all copyright holders, but if any have been overlooked the publisher will be pleased to include any necessary credits in any subsequent reprint or edition.

For further information on Polity, visit our website:
politybooks.com

To Aijun, Ada, Blai and Gael.
I hope you can feel free.

And to all of you
in the struggle,
who fill my world with joy.

Contents

vii

To Be or Not to Be

It's a boy. It's a girl.

Looking at the screen I can only see a beating heart, something resembling arms, life in black and white inside my womb. But it's a boy. Or a girl.

We don't yet know if they'll like painting, if they'll prefer spaghetti to croquettes, what colour eyes they'll have, whether their hair will be blond or black. We don't know their way of smiling or crying or losing their temper or living. But we're told 'it's a boy' or 'it's a girl' and suddenly the world is divided into two possibilities and that's that – pink and blue, arts and sciences, power and beauty.

It's so automatic a process that many experiments have been conducted about a baby's supposed gender and the attitude it provokes. In one of the studies, for example, some babies were dressed in pink and others in blue, then they were shown to various people. These people described the babies dressed in pink as 'pretty, sweet, delicate, small'; those in blue as 'strong, intelligent, stubborn, big'. The babies' clothes were switched: those in pink were dressed in blue and vice versa. With its clothing changed, the same baby's characteristics magically changed too. Those who were 'small' suddenly became 'big'; those who were 'strong' suddenly became 'delicate'.

And then, much uneasiness. Once it's confirmed that the world will react differently to this unknown person depending on whether I name them Ben or Brenda, how can I make space for them to be whoever they might want to be? How do I make space for him to dress in pink if he wants, or for her to play football if it's what she likes? Or, even more complicated, how do I make space for them to discover whether they are a she, a he or a they? The answer is more worrying than the question: I can't. Socialization will come along, life will come along, and however much we insist on having clothes of all colours at home, they'll go to school and learn the box to which they have been assigned and the punishments that await them if they leave it. It'll be their job to work out whether it's worth going against the flow or whether they prefer to adjust to it and go unnoticed.

We've been so conditioned by culture that right now it's impossible for us to know which part of the division of biological sex comes from nature, which part is made up of characteristics 'naturally' shared by a sufficiently large majority of people with XX or XY chromosomes to make reasonable generalizations, and which we impose on ourselves as a society, assigning characteristics which are not innate, but forced on us by the reading of how we should be as regards our sex. Having reached this point, it's certainly undeniable that Simone de Beauvoir was completely right when she said that one isn't born, but rather becomes, a woman. And we can add that it's exactly the same for men.

When we're born (or even from the earliest ultrasound images), our external sexual organs are examined and, if there's nothing unusual, we're classified as a man or as a woman. It's a boy; it's a girl. A person's biological sex is determined by the sex organs, chromosomes and hormones they generate. If the external sexual organs are obvious, nothing further is inspected. If the group to which they belong isn't so clear, tests are done and everything else is studied.

Not everyone fits into the male box or the female box, which seems surprising because it's discussed very little, despite the fact that it's more common than we might think. There are people with XXY chromosomes; there are people with XY chromosomes who don't secrete enough testosterone or aren't sensitive to it (and therefore have external sexual organs resembling the majority of people with XX chromosomes);

there are people with XX chromosomes who secrete more testosterone than usual (and therefore can develop certain secondary characteristics resembling those of the majority of people with XY chromosomes); and a thousand other variations. This group of people with such diverse characteristics *have to fit into* the man group or the woman group at all costs, because our society doesn't allow any alternative.

Thousands of people with intersex conditions (or differences in sex development – 'DSD' for short) from around the world endure medical (surgical or hormonal, for example) interventions to make them externally adapt to one of the labels, long before they are able to give consent. The thinking behind this is that there's been a 'mistake' in nature which needs to be corrected. But, in truth, the characteristics of intersex people don't interfere with their health (as interventions do). They don't have an illness that needs to be cured. Nowadays, many intersex people who have reached adulthood ask that these children's bodies be respected and any interventions put off until they're old enough to ask for them and give informed consent. We'd do well to listen to them.

When we're born, we're assigned either of the only two possible sexes. Even from a legal point of view, being classified is imperative: otherwise, in most states around the world, we can't be added to the civil register. If it's unclear whether it's a boy or a girl, we have to make it up. The doctors propose something based on the results they've collected and the gender it seems will be easiest for the child to perform according to their biological characteristics, and the parents usually listen.

But even in unambiguous cases in which the three elements determining sex coincide, two things can happen when the person grows up: they agree with the diagnosis of being a boy or a girl (and then they'll be cisgender) or they don't agree and know that they're a boy even though they've been told they're a girl, or vice versa (and then they'll be transgender). It could also happen that they don't feel comfortable with either group and end up labelling themself as agender, queer, gender-fluid or non-binary. And then life gets complicated: we like simplifications (it's a boy, it's a girl) and get very nervous when someone steps out of the box. However much we state we don't want labels, we're more than that, it's no use. Strangers will place us in one of the two boxes at first glance (if you have a beard, you're a man; if you have breasts, you're a woman; if you have both, alarm bells) and they treat us accordingly, whether we agree or not.

The box is what we call 'gender': the behaviours we expect of a person according to the biological sex we assume they have – that is, the rules we learn to follow according to whether we've been told we're boys or girls. These rules have little to do with a person's abilities and preferences, and are applied not only before abilities can be expressed but before they can even be discovered. We don't give small children the chance to discover what they really like because we mercilessly apply gender restrictions that will prevent our son wearing dresses or our daughter being assertive.

You can't go to the registry office when the person you're carrying in your womb is born and say: 'Look, I don't know if it's a boy or a girl or something else entirely; they don't know how to talk yet and I don't know them at all.' And determining whether a person 'is' a boy or girl is not only legally, but socially, imperative. The few instances where families have decided not to publicly communicate the biological sex of their baby, in an attempt to avoid putting the pressures of gender on them and to allow the child to develop unhindered by stereotypes and prejudices, have provoked all kinds of judgment directed at the parents. Why don't they let them 'be normal'? How should these babies be treated? Do I refer to them as 'him' or 'her'? Doesn't calling them 'they' sound ridiculous?

It's a boy. It's a girl. I know how I need to treat them. It's reassuring. We don't want to abandon the available boxes, and perhaps, given how the system is structured, abandoning them isn't reasonable, but greater flexibility between them would be very good for everyone. If I'm classified as a woman, but all that follows from this 'being a woman' is the possibility that in the future I might have the physical ability to become pregnant, and everything else is left open, I'll have the freedom to discover myself. On the other hand, if my bedroom has already been painted pink and a pile of dolls bought for me before I was born, and as I start to grow I'm told 'that's not for girls' when I stray from the norm, it'll be harder to know whether I like pink because it's pretty or because I've been force-fed it.

Research has shown that the favorite colours of babies younger than 1 are blue and red. Some babies prefer blue and others red, but there is no division by sex. Pink is of little interest – nor are grey and brown. However, by the age of 4, girls show an undeniable preference for pink, and boys avoid it at all costs. By then, they've had time to learn which group they belong to and what their colour is. Furthermore, the girls have learned to respect the codes of the colour blue, even though it's not theirs, and the boys have learned to disparage pink.

Almost everything can be generalized in this way. The most intrepid girls quickly learn to repress themselves, and the most fearful boys to be brave. Only the people who, for whatever reason, have more difficulty in acting as is expected of them find themselves forced to seek other paths, which will never be easy. The boys with hobbies that are considered feminine, whether it is dancing or experimenting with hair and make-up, have to endure taunts and insults even now – just like the girls with hobbies considered masculine.

In this book, the words 'men' and 'women' don't refer to a person's biological sex, not even their gender expression, because we know there are many more than two possibilities. We're talking about the set of expectations society has for people classified as a man or a woman, and the rules applied to them. When we say 'Women shoulder the greater part of the duties in the traditional family', we mean 'Society expects the people categorized as women to shoulder the greater part of duties in the traditional family.' When we say 'Men earn 24 per cent more than women', we mean 'The average salary of people categorized as men is 24 per cent higher than that of the people categorized as women.'

We know that there are infinite different ways of living: there are men who earn less than some women, there are women more aggressive than some men, and we know that there are people who don't consider themselves man or woman and don't know where they sit. But we also know that there are privileges enjoyed and discriminations suffered depending on which label falls to you, and that label is placed on you without you asking. This is what we're talking about, with generalizations as necessary as they are realistic.

It's a boy. It's a girl. The impossibility of being you, whoever you may be, and being treated as a person, full stop, whoever you may be. It's a boy; it's a girl. When they'd really like to be just a heart beating in all the colours that exist.

Machine Guns

My fantasy is a machine gun.

When I'm on the street and a stranger shouts something at me: a machine gun.

When the typical politician makes a typically sexist remark: a machine gun.

When a newspaper quotes a bishop who wonders how women expect not to be raped if they ask for free, unrestricted abortion: a machine gun.

When a father attending parents' evening is praised to the skies, but the mother attending is taken for granted: a machine gun.

When they fire you because you're pregnant: a machine gun.

When they tell me not to get worked up, it's no big deal: a machine gun.

It may seem like a violent fantasy, but it's not; it's a fantasy of self-defence. An act of aggression provokes a response. The response must be proportionate to be considered self-defence, you'll say. Is it proportionate to pull out a machine gun because someone makes a sexist remark? Certainly not. But what is an ocean of oppression if not a sea of drops of injustice?

It's a pleasant fantasy because there's no will to carry it out in practice: I can live it in my head without blood on my hands, without guts on my shoes, without having to consider whether the person before me deserves my accumulated rage. I don't have a machine gun, nor do I want one. I just want the right to imagine it.

This right is one that has always been denied to me. It's always been calls to give in, shut up, pay no mind, for as long as I can remember.

When boys at school lifted our skirts: Boys will be boys, ignore it.

When I was 15 and complained about street harassment: Pretend you don't hear them.

When I got home after a group of boys cornered me one evening: Don't walk down that street again.

No one ever said: 'Defend yourself.' No one ever said: 'Give 'em a smack.' Everyone always told me to take responsibility for avoiding other people's aggression.

To leave the area or, even worse, put up with the aggression and see it as natural. No one offered to find a machine gun and protect me. In fact, those who were supposed to protect me punished me if I wasn't friendly enough, if they thought I lacked charm or submissiveness.

The narrative of the good girl who doesn't vex, who is always well mannered, who under no circumstances resorts to violence, is killing women. It makes them tolerate and accept as normal assaults deemed unacceptable when committed against men. And, on the other hand, it makes them repress responses considered completely normal in men.

A French team recorded a (young, attractive) man descending an escalator winking, blowing kisses at and sometimes momentarily touching the hand of unknown men who were ascending. The vast majority of men approached reacted in a violent manner, insulting him and even hitting him, until they discovered there was a hidden camera. Then the actor stated that he had no sexual interest in those he'd approached and they enacted some kind of reaffirmation of their masculinity, like shaking hands or slapping each other's backs.

Very few of them turned away and left without insulting him. Men aren't accustomed to being sexually propositioned by strangers in public spaces. They're not accustomed to being treated as objects, not accustomed to their desire not being taken into account and another's being imposed on them. Confronted by a desire they don't share, they become violent.

Besides, they must protect their masculinity. If another man makes advances on them and they don't react negatively, it could be interpreted as proof that they're gay. One of the pillars of masculinity is obligatory heterosexuality, assumed by default. Furthermore, the image of the dominant male is reinforced by the active search for 'prey'. Becoming another man's 'prey' is intolerable. Telling someone on the street what you think of their physique isn't in pursuit of connection, it's a display of dominance.

Perhaps those who'll go on to be men have been taught to react too quickly, but it's clear that we encourage those who'll go on to be women to develop an extremely high threshold of tolerance of aggression. This has got to the point that we need campaigns spelling out that physical violence is not the only form of abuse. For many, physical attacks are the only 'real' ones. Women have been taught to pretend that nothing is wrong and have made it into a survival strategy. Women normalize lack of respect and aggression and keep doing what they were doing, as happily as they can. Women grow very thick skins.

The machine gun fantasy is therefore an aspirational one: for me, educated to be a woman, it's not my place to dream of machine guns. My place is to dream of restorative embraces, the transforming power of love, meeting a tortured man and healing his wounds with my goodness. If I can suffer a little along the way, even better. Even more redemptive.

On the other hand, the machine gun allows me to make a man disappear once I've given up on him (there's no magic solution for the hopeless cases), and reassures me that at least this particular person won't re-offend. But it's subversive because it means responding with their weapons, forbidden to me not only in practice but also in theory. A woman dreaming of a machine gun is subversive in itself. That's how bad things are.

Perhaps films in which a conventionally attractive girl (never a woman) with scant clothing and ample justifications for violence expertly wields a machine gun come to mind. Don't be fooled: the fantasy in this case is for males, who can always control her if they're real men. My fantasy isn't to become Lara Croft, it's to shut a sexist lowlife up forever.

In my fantasy, the machine gun weighs nothing – it appears magically in my hands when needed and I'm never traced by the police. No one suffers and the corpse happily evaporates from the scene: from the doctor's surgery, from the office, from the TV, from wherever there had previously been a sexist. In my fantasy, the sexist isn't a person, just as I'm not a person in his eyes.

But if the machine gun can never be more than a fantasy, how should I react to everyday aggressions? The way I've been taught? Most of the time, yes. It's more practical to pretend you don't hear them, especially when you don't know the speaker. But sometimes there's a drop that makes the glass overflow or some random guy is trying to be really 'hilarious', or I'm simply feeling stronger than usual. And then I grab my private machine gun, which is speaking 'out of turn' and even using swear words.

Here my fantasy ends and his discomfort begins: they read me as a woman, and a woman who doesn't shut up and doesn't accept his comments is unsettling. A woman saying "Don't interrupt me, I'm not finished' may not be a shot to the head, but the effect is like pouring a jug of cold water over patronizing males who think that deigning to half-listen to you, even though you're not one of their mates, makes them ultra-openminded and ultra-egalitarian. Saying 'Who asked you what you think of my body? Want me to rate your bald head?' when they call you a 'good girl' doesn't usually solve anything and can still lead to insults, but at the very least it breaks the established pattern. It makes the idea that 'I can say whatever I like to a woman with no consequences' falter, however minimal the consequences may be.

We who were educated to be submissive women subvert the established order when we speak instead of staying quiet. As we learnt in childhood, this carries sanctions. Once in adulthood, however, we can evaluate whether these sanctions are powerful enough to keep us quiet. Most of the time, there's no serious sanction attached to raising your voice. In the best of cases, you unsettle a sexist; in the worst, they insult you. And we're already used to being insulted.

When we speak instead of staying quiet, a common response is a call for order, often with the command 'Calm down.' It's not the one speaking who's worked up, but the one being spoken to, who isn't used to being stopped in his tracks or having his privileges pointed out. The call for calm is an attempt to suppress normally legitimate expression, wanting women nice and quiet because they're prettier that way (but they end up more dead that way).

My machine gun fantasy is my treasure. My way of saying 'This mind is mine'; my way of saying 'You won't subdue me.' Even more important: it's my way of being free to imagine violence and, at the same time, choosing to act differently.

Not All Men

One of the most common ripostes from men when talking about the injustices women suffer is 'I don't do anything like that.' Say most domestic duties fall to women and it won't be long before a man states that he does the ironing at home, as if one case – or even a thousand – wipes out the global statistics.

We know there's no absolute truth and luckily many men are working to deconstruct the ruling model of masculinity and become well-rounded people. Even so, why are there so many men who feel the need to attack the facts by using themselves as a shining example of manhood, instead of recognizing that they are the exception that proves the rule?

When they say 'Not all men are like that', they're not contributing to what could be an enriching dialogue highlighting different models of masculinity

– they simply want to deny that discrimination exists, which is just another way of discriminating. Many base it on their own background, which is completely valid as lived experience but irrelevant in light of the studies that demonstrate structural discrimination time and again. When we cite the fact that, on average, women dedicate 23 hours a week to domestic work and men only 7, or that 15 per cent of fathers don't do any housework at all, we're not denying that there are some men who do everything at home, but they're clearly the exception. Wanting to use an exceptional instance to refute contrasting data isn't only fallacious; it demonstrates lack of respect for those who are familiar with the subject and have taken pains to document it.

Another common reaction is to point to men also suffering discrimination for being men, or suffering the same discrimination women do. Again, it's obvious that not all women are more oppressed than all men; a rich white woman in a European country almost certainly has a better life than a poor Black man in the same country.

However, in no instance do men suffer the same discrimination or in the same proportion as women. Even more importantly, let's remind ourselves once more that they have a monopoly on violence. Some men are raped, this we know, but the number is nowhere near as high as the number of women.

Furthermore, both men and women are mostly raped by men.

On the other hand, a violent woman can't rely on a system that legitimizes her behaviour in the same way that a violent man can. If a woman hits her partner, she's subverting a social norm, while a man beating his partner is upholding it.

The idea that women are also violent but express violence 'differently', or even 'worse' than men, is perverse. According to data from the UN, the majority of violent crimes are committed by men. Women have not only been denied recourse to physical violence, but are even singled out as having inappropriately angry responses in contexts where it is legitimate to feel rage.

The manipulative woman who wraps her man around her little finger by using sex or tears is sold to us as abhorrent, but this doesn't take into account that in many cases it's the only defence remaining in a society that has denied women any other way of achieving their goals. They're valued exclusively as sexual objects for the pleasure of men, but sanctioned when they use sex as a currency. They're considered weak, inferior beings, but blamed when they display weakness to obtain more favourable treatment. That is, they're not permitted to play with the same weapons, and punished when they make use of others.

Another pet remark when talking about sexism is: 'Women are worse.' It's undeniable that sexist women exist: the patriarchal system couldn't be sustained without the collaboration of 51 per cent of the population. But how can a sexist woman be worse than a sexist man? Shouldn't they at least be equal? A sexist man enjoys all the privileges associated with being a man. A sexist woman has the lamentable role of helping to perpetuate a system which oppresses her. On the other hand, not everyone can afford the luxury of deconstruction. Questioning the established order requires a distance more easily acquired when you have education, time and information within reach. When a sexist woman comes to understand that she's playing for the enemy, it's likely she'll want to change. In contrast, there are many men who, even as they see the injustice of the system, don't lift a finger to transform it. It's more comfortable for them to lean on tradition, they're afraid of being punished if they report instances of inequality, or they perceive that a more egalitarian society would go directly against their personal interests. In my view, these are the worst: those who are fully aware of these inequalities and are perpetuating them out of self-interest.

As is so often the case, women are blamed for the wrongs done to them. If they're raped, it's because they wear short skirts; if they're abused, it's because they allow it; if society is sexist, it's because they permit it.

But actually, they're raped because there are rapists, they're abused because there are abusers, and society is sexist because the system of alienation is so brutal it makes us believe it's natural and there's no way to change it, just as 'There's always been poor people and rich people' is used to justify class inequality.

When we condemn sexism, we're not attacking any man in particular, or even men in general. We understand that we don't replicate sexist attitudes because we're bad people, but because we find them normal. We've normalized inequality and it takes a lot to escape it. But if anything is to change, women must stop being afraid to flag inequalities, and men must stop defending themselves as if it is a personal affront.

We must contribute to the change, starting by being open to listening. If you're a man and being told that discrimination exists in the workplace bothers you, why do you think it bothers you? All indicators suggest there is discrimination. Do you think it brings your salary or workplace into question? If you believe you've got there solely on personal merit and in no instance counted on the advantages that come with being a man, aren't you deceiving yourself? What have you done to avoid benefitting from the bias in your favour? Isn't thinking that there's certainly no woman in the world who deserves this job more than you a sexist attitude?

If seeing your own privilege is hard, it's precisely because it's been absorbed so deeply that it seems logical. I'd never considered how peacefully I walk down the street (by day at least) until a Maghrebi friend told me that the police stop him two or three times a week asking for his ID. I've never been stopped. Precisely because I've never been stopped, I hadn't even considered that this could happen. If, instead of saying 'Damn, I hadn't thought about it, I'm so sorry' to my friend, I were to say 'It's no big deal, just show your ID – done', wouldn't that be racist? Wouldn't I be oppressing him even more? Or am I assuming that the fact that I've never been stopped has nothing to do with my race but everything to do with the fact that I'm a good person and it shows?

The other side of the same coin is when men displaying non-sexist attitudes or those who vindicate feminism are celebrated. Just as a woman declaring herself a feminist is immediately suspect, a man calling himself one generates curiosity at the very least, if not admiration. When a man repeats an idea said ad infinitum by feminists, suddenly it gains new relevance. Perhaps if he's saying it, it must be more true, to begin with, because he's a man and men have more prestige. But deep down there's another, even more worrying, idea: men don't stand to gain anything from feminism, so if they support it they must be admired for their altruism.

Actually, men stand to gain a lot from feminism. For one thing, the freedom to explore who they are without discrimination for not following the rules of masculinity. But, even if it weren't so, defending equal rights and practical opportunities for everyone should be the most normal thing in the world, whoever you are. Why should we give medals to the men who restrain themselves from attacking human rights? Shouldn't we expect men to treat women (and everyone generally) with respect?

Some male newcomers to the feminist movement have so deeply absorbed the dynamics of leadership that they feel compelled to explain to women with years of experience how the fight should be led. To my mind, men are more than welcome to join the feminist struggle, but it must be led by women. If a key feminist assertion is that they're not in the room when decisions are taken, why should they also cede decision-making power about how to deal with misogynistic discrimination to men?

On the other hand, there are those who behave as if demanding a certain right for women also means depriving men of it. History has shown that this isn't so: when the suffragettes obtained the women's right to vote, men didn't lose it. It simply became a universal right.

What we do demand is the abolition of privilege. In print journalism, 80 per cent of newspaper columnists are men. Clearly, if we're seeking 50:50 parity, many men will have to give up being column-ists. But this in no way goes against men's right to have a public voice in the media; it simply corrects a historic over-representation. Up to now they've had more of a platform than they were entitled to, and this has violated women's right to media representa-tion. Balancing the situation so every gender has its share is logical.

The adverse reaction to ceding a share of power is visceral. Someone who has always been given three oranges is suddenly only given two, because the other is being given to the person who used to receive only one. Rather than recognizing historic injustice, many demand three oranges, regardless of whether the dis-tribution is fair or not. Since they've always received them, they're convinced of their right to have three and accuse the other person of stealing what is theirs. They don't see that they were the ones who were 'stealing' until now.

Every time gender quotas are discussed, we hear that, if we applied them, we'd have to do the same for sexual orientation, race, disability, etc. And, in fact, why not? If we truly choose the best person for each job, aside from privilege, statistically the result must be parity in all aspects. If at heart we believe that only the best reach the top, and that by chance the best person in every field is a white man with a more or less normative body of a certain age and social class, we have a profound bias issue. Quotas are only one of the corrective measures for this bias and must be accompanied by policies that ensure equal opportunities and rights for all people – that is, intersectional feminist policies.

Accepting that not all men are the same means accepting there are men who are intelligent and not so intelligent, sexist and not so sexist, fair and not so fair. But this doesn't take away from the fact that all men, just because they're men, have it easier than a woman of the same class, racial minority, orientation, disability, etc.

Until men clearly see the extent to which they are privileged by the system, they cannot be true comrades in the struggle. The only logical response to the statement 'Not all men are the same' is 'Thank our lucky stars!'

Raped Bodies, Rapable Bodies

If the clichéd image of rape were true and, once raped, a woman would never go outside again, the world would come to a standstill, because there are very few women who have never suffered sexual assault. Women wouldn't be able to go out to work or do the laundry. They wouldn't be able to take children to school or go to the cinema. They wouldn't be able to do anything but stay in bed depressed, or drug themselves up to the eyeballs, or kill themselves, as films inform us must be done after being raped. Luckily, that isn't really how it goes.

I'm astonished by the number of friends who have been raped. Almost all by men they knew. Partners, above all. Fathers. Grandfathers. Uncles. Cousins. Brothers. I'm astonished by the number of friends who only talk about it once another woman has let it slip, usually after hours of discussing other things, usually when we've been drinking.

I'm astonished that it's taken years for so many to understand that what happened was rape. One friend explains that her boyfriend forced her to when she didn't feel like it, and she ended up feeling violated. Another tells her that it's rape if she didn't want to and he went ahead anyway. A third woman's expression suddenly changes. And yes, they recognize that anguish, the fear, the disgust, the desire for it to end. All mixed with so much love. They love their men and their men love them, or so they believe. If one thing is clear, it's that women are taught to love badly.

All these friends, all these unknown females who have been raped, are normal women. They are women of all kinds who do all kinds of things, who laugh and dance and get angry and get frustrated. They are happy and unhappy women. They are. They're making do. They keep going.

According to data from the Fundació Vicky Bernadet [Vicky Bernadet Foundation], 23% of women (and 17% of men) have suffered sexual abuse as a minor. According to the Mossos d'Esquadra [Police Squad of Catalonia], 96% of those reporting sexual assalts are women (the majority between 13 and 37 years of age) and 100% of the attackers are men.

The incidents reported are the tip of the iceberg: not one of my friends who have been raped reported it. Generally, we live it, we come to terms with it, we keep going. It's more often reported when the rapist is a stranger, which only happens in some 20% of cases. But if it's someone you know, reporting it means having to explain to those closest to you that that man who is so nice and so normal, who might live in your house, who you might depend on financially, or who might be the life and soul of the party, has done something unimaginable.

Rarely do families take the part of the one attacked. That man is not a stranger who goes down the street in a balaclava, not an unhinged psychopath, not a disgusting being. He's usually the father of a family, and it's a pity that most people haven't read Hannah Arendt nor even know that the father of the family is the great criminal of the twentieth century (and this hasn't improved in the twenty-first, I'm afraid). It's very hard for the families to admit that someone they love has hurt someone else they also love, just as it is for the victim herself.

The lawyers of Dones Juristes [Women Lawyers] explain that the judicial process usually takes over two years, during which time the complainant will be continually questioned. Not only by those around her and the media, if the news leaks out (What was she wearing? What was she doing around there at that time? Why didn't she report it before?), but by the very participants in the process. Police officers attend the hospital three or four hours after a rape, when the woman is still in shock. Judges and prosecutors don't understand if she happens to remember what happened in more detail later on.

How do you respond to a lawyer who asks you if you closed your legs when they tried to rape you? If you were paralyzed, if you were scared and preferred to make it easier, if it was someone you trusted, if you didn't want to make him angry, if you thought it was your duty, if you were unable to react in any other way – how do you make someone who hasn't lived through it understand? And why should you have to close your legs? What was that man doing forcing you to open them? Why do we think it natural that, unless a woman violently opposes it, she's consenting to sex? What kind of animals are we that accept that sex can occur without looking the other person in the eye, without noticing how their body responds, without being completely sure that the pleasure is mutual? When lawyers explain how the judicial process will go, the majority of women who wanted to file a report pull out. This is yet another job women have: being judged for a crime someone else has committed.

I'm astonished by the number of friends who have been raped because this means I must have at least some friends and certainly a fair number of acquaintances who are rapists, and that's worrying. But I'm even more astonished by the number of friends who have escaped it. By using various tactics, they've on various occasions found a way of stopping horrible attempts to invade their bodies. They're not seen in statistics or in films, nor is it widely discussed outside private circles. It's hard to put a number on them, but there are many around me.

The one who found herself cornered by the gasman and somehow managed to say 'Your mother wouldn't be too happy about what you're doing to me', after which he sprang back, apologized and left. The one who opened the door to find a knife pointing at her, and, with a surge of adrenaline stronger than she'd ever felt before, grabbed the idiot by the T-shirt, lifted him into the air and threw him out into the street. The one who was followed when she left the nightclub and, when they told her not to make a sound and to get into the car, broke into a run and escaped. Me too, at just 14 years old, when I shoved my stepfather away and locked myself in my room after he'd cornered me in the kitchen.

For many years, I've wondered what stopped him, that day I came home from school and he was there – I don't remember why – at a time when no one else was at home. I think it was a mix of surprise (he didn't expect me not to let him), a guilty conscience (if I didn't let him, did I not want to?) and fear (if I didn't want to, would I tell my mother?). At any rate, acting as if I wasn't a vulnerable young girl, in front of an adult who should have protected me instead of raping me, saved me that evening.

Where are the films showing women defending themselves? Winning a battle, if not the war? Where are the films in which they don't remain paralyzed, not screaming, defenceless – that for a moment over-look the fact that they belong to the weaker sex and their role is to shut up and swallow?

Even the wimpiest of men is backed by centuries of oppression in which the dirty work's been done for him. Women have been convinced that there is no possibility of fighting. I don't mean fighting as a duty to keep the body inviolable, as if it were a sanctuary that must be offered to a more or less chosen male, but fighting for the right to their own space, if they are able – because sometimes they would be able if they didn't believe they weren't. Fighting to use their bodies as they please, offering it to whomever they please, if they please.

Rape, which is a temporary occupation of the body, begins with the permanent occupation of the mind. The absurd cliché in films must be forgotten. If you happen upon him in a dark alley and manage to over-come your (legitimate, of course) fear, take a good look at him. He's also alone. And maybe he's not that strong or that big. Maybe if you surprise him, disorientate him, you can escape. He doesn't know it, but he should be afraid of you. At the end of the day, you're both in a dark alley – there's no one else there. The abundant adrenaline coursing through your veins could hurt him badly.

I know too well that we're not all lucky enough to react this way, that fear is an effective poison and that your body can betray you, that you can lack the will even to breathe. The right to defend yourself must under no circumstances become the obligation to defend yourself. Why didn't I close my legs? Because I couldn't. Why did I punch him? Because I could. Any reaction must be possible. Raping must be the only inadmissible thing, not being raped or defending oneself against being raped.

However, the image seared into our minds is that of the vulnerable woman. In any television series – low-budget or high-end, good or bad – there comes the episode in which a degenerate rapes a girl. It's almost inevitable: the girl cannot defend herself. He is stronger, scarier. There's no one around, it's dark, and it makes no difference whether she screams or not: no one hears her, no knight in shining armour is coming to rescue her. So it goes, and she ends up committing suicide or becoming a drug addict or no longer having a sex life. In the best of cases, she becomes a serial killer of rapists. Few – very, very few – get over it and live a 'normal' life, as mostly happens in reality.

And like this, with images that are difficult to forget, we're persuaded that our bodies are not ours: they belong to whoever might want to rob us of them. We're persuaded that we're weak, that they always win, that it's better not to resist too much and that way maybe they won't kill us. And not only that: staying home, not going out alone, not drinking too much, staying alert are offered to us as alternatives to rape. It's always on women not to provoke the ferocious beast supposedly inside men (What were you wearing? Why were you around there at that time? Why didn't you report it before? Did you close your legs?). But if men have a run-of-the-mill uncontrollable beast within, how come they don't rape in all circumstances? How come they know how to control it when they're likely to get caught, or with women they don't think will keep quiet? How do they choose their victims so well? Furthermore, how come there are men who never rape anyone?

One element contributing to the fact that men aren't raped as much as women is the construction of their bodies as unrapable. In popular imagination, women, children and homosexuals (who aren't considered 'real' men) can be raped, but not men. The only depiction of male rape we have is of prison, in which an exclusively male population must find those who are 'less manly' to satisfy the sexual urges of those who are 'more manly'.

Women grow up with warnings about how they must avoid provoking males, because it is taken for granted that it's not necessary for men to avoid provoking anyone. The (false) assumption that rape is about sexuality, when it's actually a matter of power, exempts women, who are devoid of any sexual desire other than what men feel for them. Likewise, if you're a man and another man rapes you, it's because you're not man enough. If you're 'man enough' you needn't fear anyone.

As is the case for raped women, raped men are blamed for the assault, but, while being rapable is considered an intrinsic characteristic of a woman's body, that of a man has to be unrapable, the price being that the masculinity of the few men who admit to being raped is brought into question. Therefore, there's an additional incentive for men not to report the rapes they suffer.

On the other hand, the coitocentric idea which teaches us that a man penetrating someone is the only sexual relation possible, and therefore also the only rape possible, makes it seem inconceivable that (cisgender) women could rape. Instances of sexual abuse in which an adult woman abuses a minor are not considered rape, but 'initiations'. Many men who suffered sexual abuse by adult women when they were 13 or 14 years old see the abuse as their first consensual sexual relationship, even though the age of consent around the world is commonly 16.

Because there's sometimes a desire to see the lines as more blurred than they really are, it must be remembered that any sexual contact by an adult with anyone younger than 16 is a crime. Furthermore, any sexual contact in which there is deception on the part of an adult or they hold a position of trust, authority or influence over a minor is considered sexual abuse, even if the minor is over 16. And it's very difficult for an adult not to be in a position of trust, authority or influence over a minor.

There's a fantasy among adolescent boys of 'fucking a friend's mother or a female teacher', as if the man (or in this case, the boy) must always have the power in a sexual relationship, and as if other factors of privilege such as experience, the teacher–student power dynamic, or economic power and the capacity for informed choice don't count at all, regardless of what the law says.

It might be considered a good thing that this view of relationships sidesteps the trauma of being abused for many men, but it's actually a way of oppressing them. For all the male privilege they have, boys and adolescent males should be able to develop their sexuality as freely as girls and adolescent females, and sexual and emotional education must make everyone recognize the limits in relationships between grown-ups and minors. And, for that matter, it should help us construct the idea that no body is rapable, rape is intolerable and there are serious consequences to going beyond the limits of consent.

Misfits

'I've never felt discriminated against as a woman' is a phrase that reveals exactly how effective conditioning is: there are some who have so completely normalized oppression that they don't see it as a negative. When a friend says this to me, I ask whether she's ever had her behind touched on the Underground, or ever been patronized by male colleagues at work. The answer is usually yes, it's happened to them at least once.

'But it doesn't bother me, idiots exist and you have to deal with it.' And the system triumphs once more: getting us to believe that men and women suffer equally at the hands of 'people' in general who are idiots.

As we've seen before, according to data from the UN, the majority of crimes are committed by men. Even though it varies by country and type of crime, men commit between five and ten times more crimes than women, especially when referring to violent and/or sexual crimes. Yes, both men and women are victims, but they're victims of different crimes. Many more women are raped, and in contrast more men are killed, but women are killed by the men closest to them (partner, ex-partner, acquaintances) and men are killed by strangers. That is, the criminals are usually men and we suffer differently depending on whether we're seen as men or women.

On the other hand, there are all the assaults that don't end up being reported. If there was a report every time a man touches a woman's behind on the Underground, the police force would collapse. Women learn to take them as things that happen, they try not to make too much of them. They'll be late for school or work, they don't have time to raise hell.

Everything that isn't assault, but simple disrespect, also needs to be considered. When your appearance but not your competence is appraised in the workplace; when in a mixed group the men pretend the women don't exist and speak only among themselves; when you don't laugh at a sexist joke and your sense of humour is questioned rather than the poor taste of the joke . . .

Declaring that you've never felt discriminated against as a woman means you have a high tolerance for oppression and you've normalized habitual harassment, not that you're not discriminated against. It's a logical defence mechanism, allowing you not to waste energy on continual (and often useless) confrontations, but it aims to render invisible a problem which will continue to be there even if you want to deny it. What's more, a woman who upholds this idea is immediately applauded by men: she earns validation and is considered as 'more equal' through the simple fact of denying an inequality few wish to see. Validation from men carries more social prestige than the support of other women.

Women who feel most comfortable with the roles they're required to develop, who have taken on this lower status, who have come to believe that the division of two genders with totally different values, rights and duties is natural and even fair, are those who don't see the need to change anything. Even though the value system they're defending objectively punishes them (to give just one example, discrimination in the workplace does exist, independent of one's personal perception), their confronting it would exact a higher personal cost than accepting it.

The more comfortable you are in the cage of patriarchy, the more you contribute to reinforcing it. This same process explains why – even though in many ways patriarchy also oppresses men – there are vastly more feminist women than feminist men. It offers men such advantages that losing them isn't worth it for the majority, even in exchange for being more free.

So why are there some who fight inequality? Well, because the system isn't perfect and, despite all its perpetuating mechanisms, there are more and more individuals made uncomfortable by it. Giving up the social approval implied by fitting into the role that falls to you, at least in appearance, has a very high personal cost. Your family doesn't always understand that you don't want a partner or have a non-normative sexual orientation. You may have problems finding work if your gender expression doesn't fit the norm. You might even be beaten for being out in public in clothes that 'aren't meant for you'.

The vast majority of people uncomfortable within the system try as hard as possible to fit into it, but it's not always easy. The more legal equality we achieve, but without gaining equality in practice, and the more it's insisted that practical equality exists even though it's a lie, the more women there are who collide with an unsatisfactory reality.

Among the women of our generation, told at school that they were equal to their male classmates, there's a sense of being completely taken in: the world hasn't changed as much as they'd hoped, nor are they in as good a position as they should be by this point. Furthermore, however much you're convinced that you're worth it, that you want it, that you can do it, decision-makers are sceptical and the so-called 'glass ceiling' is painfully real.

Their partners, who should have changed nappies and cleaned toilets and passionately discussed everything with them, have preferred to settle into traditional roles. The majority of my female friends who have a heterosexual partner concur in the diagnosis: the moment you get distracted, the apron and baby are palmed off on you and they're off to watch sports with their friends.

Women are the guardians of equality because it's not to men's benefit, and if they're not superheroes of consistency and magnanimity, being a traditional male isn't only practical, it's even acceptable. In male friendship groups, those who take on their domestic and childrearing responsibilities are often teased and likely called 'hen-pecked'. That is, being responsible is being less of a man.

It's understandable, then, that many men are seeking to escape and that women feel duped. Women have equality laws that aren't fulfilled, they're under-represented in all areas of power, the wage gap continues at an unrelenting 24 per cent, and the burden (and the joy) of childrearing isn't shared as much as they'd like.

Inequalities are more oppressive among the lowest incomes. The domestic burden of cleaning and attending to children and the unwell that women are expected to take on can be contracted out to poorer women if the necessary resources are available, partially removing the pressure on women who belong to families with greater powers of acquisition. But the cleaning ladies who liberate them from the slavery of the home also bear the weight of their own home afterwards and they can't contract it out to anyone.

Oppressions accumulate and the more they are suffered, the less liveable they make the status quo. If you're a poor, non-white, non-heterosexual, migrant woman with a physical disability, it's much more likely that the world will be more hostile to you than if you're a rich, white, heterosexual man born in the West with a normative body. . .

Many of the women who declare that they don't experience discrimination are precisely those who can pay other women to do domestic and childrearing tasks, have been able to access tertiary education, have contacts who find them more favourable jobs . . . that is, those who enjoy almost every privilege.

But the world being hostile towards you isn't enough of a condition for you to rebel against it. You'll also require a whole series of resources: a certain level of reflection on the causes of oppression, the time to deal with it and awareness of your personal agency, among many others.

However, being at least aware of the level of hostility that – if not you – others may face is indeed a necessary condition. The most empathetic people needn't experience discrimination in their own skin to fight against it, but it's easier to see when you suffer it.

The rise of female musicians such as Mala Rodríguez or Bad Gyal, who sit within genres like rap or dancehall where they coexist with many artists who sing sexist lyrics, is an interesting phenomenon. Immediately, their names, 'mala' and 'bad', flaunt their refusal to be good girls. They're perfectly aware of their transgression. Their lyrics talk about women who refuse to be trampled on, who make use of violence, who get what they want.

Their lyrics aren't necessarily feminist, but they do break the norm of 'good manners'. They express the oppression implied in 'being good girls' and propose breaking this imposed role. They don't want to be nice: a characteristic part of their public persona is the complete opposite.

Niceness is a quality valued in general, but one especially demanded of women. Women are educated to be pleasant, obedient, submissive. Insubordination and dissent are considered inappropriate and they're constantly pressured to smile, be pleasant, watch how they speak ... The claiming of violence made by singers like Mala Rodríguez or Bad Gyal has at least one aspect of feminism: they question an established order which hinders their survival in a very hostile environment.

This undoing of the tyranny of niceness – which is the same as saying submission – is a first step on the road to equality. To my mind, it means beginning to refuse the obligation of always pleasing in all circumstances. Once you free yourself from this obligation, it's easier to recognize the advantages it entails. Not doing things according to what's expected of you but according to your own ideas of what's reasonable brings you marvellous autonomy. The right to vote is reasonable and our grandmothers wouldn't have achieved it by being what, in that time (and even now), was considered 'nice'.

The price of being considered nice often means saying 'yes' when you want to say 'no', and enduring comments, gestures and even harassment that men don't suffer – or that make them hit the roof when they do – all without complaint.

The word 'feminist' is associated with notions of antagonism, rage, frustration – with reason, I think. Only a woman ready to pay the price of complaining and not being liked, ready not to be nice in all circumstances, can declare themself overtly feminist. Systematic inequality naturally generates rage and frustration, and it's precisely that rage and frustration that push them to action. There are no feminists satisfied with the world.

The idea of the bitter woman doesn't neatly fit reality. Quite the opposite: fighting for one's ideals, finding fellow women (and even a fellow or two) in the struggle, winning a small victory from time to time – all this offers fulfilment not found in accepting submission, however comfortable the gilded cage you're shut in might be.

People who see their vision of the world attacked by the feminist idea of practical equality of rights and opportunities fall back on a defence mechanism as old as it is unjust: the ad hominem fallacy. Apart from using a fallacy which literally means 'against the man' as a weapon to delegitimize feminism, there are further ironies. To start with, the irony that the first insults that come to mind are 'ugly', 'dried-up cunt' and 'whore': all three are examples of patriarchal demands on women (being attractive and desirable but restrained in putting her sexuality into practice). The majority of insults reserved for feminists alone justify the existence of feminism.

In a society where beauty is the most highly esteemed quality in a woman, calling her 'ugly' is a way of denying any relevant role she might have. The obligation to be pretty, or at least to try not to be ugly, is also related to the obligation to please others (and the others are always men). The existence of women who reject this obligation is worrying for the guardians of the system. In fact, 'ugly' is one of the first insults learned at school, way before 'whore' or 'prude', which will come later.

So, if you're fat, you're obliged to diet and exercise to slim down, regardless of whether it will help you to be healthier or not. In fact, a large number of the diets to which women subject themselves are harmful to health, not to mention the eating disorders caused by the requirement to be thin. We have ever younger girls with anorexia and bulimia, which used to emerge in adolescence and now appear at the age of 8, or even 7. Of those affected by eating disorders, 90% are mid-puberty girls when they enter the meat market and are mercilessly evaluated according to trouser and bra size. Even though the causes of these disorders are complex, we can't ignore the social rejection a fat woman arouses. The message that filters through is that your waist will never be small enough, nor your breasts large enough.

At the same time, we laugh at fat women who diet, and even more at those who exercise. On one hand, there's the obligation of trying to fit into the canons of beauty and, on the other, extreme cruelty towards those whom we know won't make it even as they try.

The exact same thing happens to women who decide to have plastic surgery. Appearing as though they're eternally under 40 is required of them, but they're punished if it's noticeable that they've gone under the knife. They're inundated with the message that women are only in the public sphere because of their appearance: they must be young and attractive.

If they're not and the magical diets, gyms and creams don't work, their friendly surgeons will 'fix' them. Then the problem is that the results don't look 'natural'. That is, there's no possible escape from criticism, because as soon as they age their wrinkles are criticized, and if they have plastic surgery they're criticized for not looking 'natural'.

There are bold people out there who dare to state that body image pressures are equal for men and women, but this only demonstrates a poor understanding of the reality. Obviously, men suffer from these expectations, but at the end of the day there's no possible comparison between the numbers of 'good-looking' women and 'good-looking' men we see on TV, in ads or at the cinema. Of the kinds of women we see in the media, the proportion that don't look like catwalk models is minuscule. It's a different thing altogether when we compare the men. This pressure is translated into an abnormal (that is, unrepresentative of the population overall) ratio of plastic surgery clients, which is 88 per cent women to 12 per cent men in Spain.

The actresses considered pretty are precisely among those who suffer the most attacks for having gone under the knife. Would we accept them having plastic surgery if they were ugly? If it's not obvious they've had surgery, do we then think it's okay if they mutilate their faces to get rid of their wrinkles? Would an actress over 40 with the face (and body) they had at 20 seem 'natural' to us? Why is it so hard for us to look at one another and accept that, yes, we've lived and it shows on our faces? That most of us aren't supermodels, nor do we need to be? That our bodies are perfectly perfect because they allow us to be alive? That our noses are fantastic if they let us breathe, that our breasts are splendid if they give us pleasure or serve to nurse our children, that our behinds are ideal if we can sit comfortably on them?

Women are pressured to look like the women in magazines, but not even they look like the versions of themselves that have been airbrushed ready for publication. They simply don't exist. The war of looks is a war we can't win, at least not in person. We'll never be thin enough, tall enough, white enough, well-groomed enough. In contrast, the majority of smartphones have automatic re-touching technology that makes your face thinner, your arms longer, or your skin smoother. The use of a filter before publishing a photo on social media is almost obligatory.

The insecurity that the obligation to aspire to an unattainable ideal creates in women is extremely profitable. This is well known by the companies that sell creams, dyes, make-up, shapewear . . . Ironically, the economic benefits from the devastation of women's self-esteem end up in the pockets of bald, pot-bellied, wrinkled business moguls.

It's a fact that beauty standards vary according to historical period and culture, and this absence of objectivity has been exploited so that we do hear 'Everyone is potentially beautiful' or – let's face it, this isn't about the men – simply 'All women are potentially beautiful.' It's an attempt to return your stolen self-confidence to you: you are actually beautiful, it's just that, right now, right here, others don't think so.

Even though recognizing the relativity of beauty can take a little of the pressure off women, it's still a fictitious relief. The pressure to be pretty, if not by the standards of this century, was still there in centuries past. But, after all, why should we want to be pretty? What evil beyond the symbolic is there in being ugly? Does it affect our health? Our ability to work? If we succeed in not letting it affect our desire to laugh and live, will we have fewer friends? Do we want friends who value only our looks?

The true revolution is not in accepting yourself as you are because you're beautiful in your own way, but accepting yourself as you are because your body allows you to live, however ugly it is. And isn't having survived to an advanced age in a hostile world a source of pride? Shouldn't the wrinkles that prove it be medals we want to show others?

'Hairy' is another common insult. Whoever is using what should be a descriptive term with pejorative intent is criticizing the fact that you aren't aspiring to suggested beauty standards. Hair is relatively easy to eliminate. If you have any where you shouldn't (and the area where you shouldn't have any keeps spreading and spreading) and don't remove it, you're not making the least effort to appear acceptably pretty. This means not only straying from the norm, but doing so *on purpose*. Not shaving underarms or legs and showing it means publicly expressing that you're not subjecting yourself to the rules. That you're not 'pretty', nor do you want to be, because the majority of women have ready access to a razor. That not pleasing men doesn't matter to you, and this is where the suspicion of homosexuality comes in.

It's clear that women are people and they have their own preferences and desires, regardless of the attraction they arouse. This seems like common sense, but is systematically denied in the images of seduction we're constantly bombarded with. Women must be pretty (or at least try to be) to please men. Whether men please them is more or less irrelevant; what matters is to please.

When a woman declares herself a feminist and therefore accepts being called disagreeable, ugly and hairy, it can only be because not pleasing men doesn't matter to her and therefore she's a lesbian. But this would mean recognizing her agency, so they go one step further and add on the suspicion that women 'turn' lesbian because they don't please men and then, resentful, become feminists.

That such childish reasoning still has a place in the twenty-first century seems incredible, but the most visceral online reactions experienced by feminists who dare to express themselves are along these lines. I don't know a single feminist activist who hasn't been told on Twitter that no one would even want to rape her (usually amid rape and death threats). Being raped isn't desirable, but sexists consider being undesirable worse than being raped, and publicly say exactly that. Luckily, the reality is that there are enough men who are, on the whole, decent for feminists to find a heterosexual partner if they want one, without much trouble. To what degree it's possible to avoid heteropatriarchal oppression within these partnerships is another question entirely. How many men are ready to give up their privileges in the private sphere? How many women are ready to never yield in the relationship, no matter how tired they are?

The initial discomfort that pushes many women towards feminism can lead to a more comfortable way of being in the world. There will be people who insult them or point out the visible signs indicating their deviance from the norm, but, with a supportive network of family and friends, they can be a little more of who they really are and a little less of what they're expected to be.

Don't Wash Your Dirty Linen in Public

A room of one's own as what Virginia Woolf wanted for writing. Writing wants time and solitude, wants calm to think, wants to drop everything for a few hours and close in on oneself. It means knowing yourself to be worthy of this time, recognizing that you have something to say and finding a voice to say it. If you also want to publish, believing that all this would interest someone else is necessary too.

Writing from a woman's point of view is a feminist act, in the sense that self-belief is required, in a way that challenges all that women have been taught they have to be. The single fact of writing already implies a respect for your own ideas that come more from within than without.

Woolf's room of one's own is symbolic and literal: what private space is left for the mother of a family? When she has finished serving others, how many hours are left to her to serve herself? There is a notion that women are no longer the slaves they used to be a few decades ago. But does this tally with reality? The data shows that there's a long way to go to reach equality within the home. The propaganda about this false, supposedly won equality is a blend of complacency and attempts to discourage the fight.

Certainly, I'm better off than my grandmother was. I can open a current account without asking any man for permission; I'm in control of whether I want children or not, and, if I do, when and how; I've had access to higher education despite my family's poverty. However, being better off isn't the same as being in an optimal situation. All these rights are due to the struggle of twentieth-century feminists and it's good to recognize them and be thankful for them, but in no way can we accept them as examples of equality: men continue to have many more freedoms than women.

The traditional family we're expected to be devoted to, which takes the form of a heterosexual couple with children, is a swindle for women. Living with a man compared to living alone means an additional hour of work per day for the woman. This seems absurd: there's not much difference between cooking for one or for two, nor cleaning a toilet used by one or by two. If everyone assumes their domestic duties, sharing a house should mean less work. However, the data shows that women finish their tasks and then have to take on a significant part of the rest. Having children isn't what gets in the way of a woman's professional career, it's living with men who consider their careers more important and their time more valuable.

According to data from the Panel de Famílies i d'Infància [Family and Childhood Commission], women spend an average of 23 hours a week on domestic chores, while men only spend 7 hours. As for the types of tasks, women work more hours on everyday tasks (looking after children, taking them to school, ironing, making meals . . .). On the other hand, the father's contribution usually focuses on tasks that don't require daily attention (taking charge of admin and fixing things around the house). The same statistics show that 51% of fathers don't do any domestic chores at all; 21% do one; 16% do two; and only 6% do three.

The famous phrase 'Behind every great man, there's a great woman,' presented to us as if it were a recognition of the task of women in the shadows, is an insult if it doesn't serve to change the situation. It means that for someone to do 'important things' – that is, triumph in the public sphere – there has to be someone else who resolves the domestic admin in the private sphere. Not only is the public sphere much more highly esteemed than the private sphere

– even though both are essential for the human race to advance – the distribution of the two spheres by gender and not by inclination or personal aptitude is also perpetuated.

Women have wanted access to the public sphere and demanded access to higher education and the workforce, but, in contrast, men haven't been interested in conquering the private sphere. Domestic labour has no social prestige and is considered secondary. So women end up toiling both outside and inside the home, with a double working day which leaves them no time for anything else.

On the other hand, the majority of the work done by men is paid work. Even though women cook at home, when cooking is made professional and becomes a field of renown, it's men who become great chefs and win awards. This isn't due to men's innate ability to cook better, but, instead, easier access to the resources which smooth the path towards success in public life.

Childrearing, of which it's expected that mothers will do a large part, needs to be added onto all these discriminations. Beyond the biological imperatives suggesting that (cisgender) women be the ones to raise the kids, mothers are required to take charge of care that could be shared. This results in the loss of more days of paid labour to tend to sick children, and all the burden of balancing (or, more precisely, the difficulty of balancing) work life and family life falling on women.

Up to now, the most important feminist milestone that has been reached is being able to choose whether to experience a pregnancy, give birth, nurse. And, if you do, when, how and with whom. This milestone isn't universal: in a large part of the world, there is no access to contraceptives and, even where there is, the social pressure to have at least one child is brutal. Those who are lucky enough to be able to turn to contraception and abortion, if necessary, don't escape the vision of motherhood as inherently feminine: being a real woman means being a mother.

The mystique around motherhood reinforces this notion. Mothers have to sacrifice everything for their children; children are the meaning of a mother's existence; without children a woman isn't 'complete'. Other sources of positive reinforcement which idealizes motherhood and causes huge frustration are ads for baby cologne in which a newborn smiles while a well-dressed, well-groomed mother caresses the baby; stories in which the mother is eternally sweet and self-sacrificing; and films in which the love for children is everything.

Even though, luckily, these things are being talked about more and more, little is said about the reality of the postpartum period, how hard the sleepless nights of the first months (or years, in some cases) are, the difficulties of organizing family life . . . Women aren't even informed about the serious consequences of pregnancy and childbirth. A packet of aspirin, which is much less harmful than gestating a baby, comes with much more information about possible side effects and contraindications than is usually received during pregnancy, or even beforehand. The physical and psychological consequences of having children are downplayed because deep down the idea that this is why women come into the world endures, and, therefore, any sacrifice is trivial. Gestating, giving birth and childrearing are what justify women's existence. It's not that important if they die or their health is damaged along the way.

Only now is the conversation beginning about 'regretful mothers', who confess that if they'd known all it entailed, they wouldn't have had children. The same question isn't put to fathers. The cost of paternity continues to be much lower, and not just physically: leaving at any time, from the beginning of the pregnancy until any moment later in the child's life, is possible. For many men, being responsible for their children is limited to making some financial contribution to the maintenance of the family and they don't even consider doing anything further. How many women who say they regret having had children wouldn't find it more satisfying if they could rely on truly responsible partners they could share the work and their concerns with?

To what point does a woman who decides to have children do so freely? How many don't end up giving in to social pressure? You must be very sure you're not drawn to the idea of motherhood, however attractively it's presented to you, to put up with the continual questioning of the choice not to have children. When you're between the ages of 30 and 40, people will keep saying things like 'Anything stirring? Your clock is ticking.' The thought that the infamous biological clock might be beating a different non-reproductive rhythm altogether doesn't occur to anyone. Not having children is a decision a cis woman retakes every day, at least until the onset of the menopause.

After all, the world doesn't appear to be set up to make a mother's life easier. Young women with children have more difficulties finding work. More difficulties than who? Obviously, young women with no children, but above all more difficulties than men, with or without children. It's taken for granted that women will be the ones to accommodate and that men don't have this problem. If men play with their children for a while or scold them from time to time when their grades are bad, they've already fulfilled their role.

What should be joint decisions about organizing how to move forward in work and life, where everyone's needs are considered and the most satisfactory solution found for everyone, become 'by default' a woman's responsibility.

Now that more and more couples are separating every day, some of my friends have expressed their envy of the separated women who share custody, because they have half the time to spend as they wish while the children's father does his share of the work. Not one male friend in a couple has expressed envy about the time the separated fathers with shared custody can spend with their children.

Unequal access to the workforce (women suffer more insecurity, with more temporary and part-time contracts than men), in addition to the wage gap (which is between 20 and 26 per cent, depending on the sources consulted) means fewer economic resources for women and greater difficulty in being self-sufficient. This greater difficulty in finding stable, well-paid, prestigious work reinforces the idea that women's careers are less important than men's.

This idea is so powerful that the former president of CEOE [the Spanish Federation of Business Organizations] Juan Rosell dared to state that: 'The inclusion of women in the workforce is a problem, because how can we create work for everyone?' Clearly, for Rosell, women don't form part of that 'everyone' worthy of having a paid job, and he was in fact thinking of 'every man', not 'every person'.

That is, if jobs are limited, men should be the first to access them. Many businessmen agree and, other things being equal, choose the male candidate.

Everything pushes women to live in coupledom: not only the social pressure which views a woman's single status as a personal failure, but above all a financial situation which makes it very difficult to pay for a room of one's own. According to the UN, women make up 70 per cent of the world's 1,300 million poorest people. For a woman in a precarious situation, being part of a heterosexual couple isn't so much a personal choice as it is a condition for survival.

This complicates personal relationships: it's difficult to establish equal relationships when domestic labour isn't valued and only done by women (or at least they organize it – that is, take responsibility for it). It's hard not to reproduce the inequalities of power that occur in the public sphere once we get home.

It's a fact that heterosexual couples with more egalitarian relationships have more satisfying and more frequent sexual relations. That is, organizing communal life on the basis of equality, as is logical, has direct repercussions on the quality of the relationship between the two. If both halves of a couple feel respected and considered, and work and leisure hours are divided equally between them, it's more likely that they are together because they choose to be and not because they have no alternative. Conjugal happiness is more easily achieved in freedom.

Homosexual couples in some countries (including Spain) have won legal recognition equal to that of heterosexual couples, with the same rights on every level. Even though this has been a huge advance and allowed many couples to legalize their situation, it has a downside: it assumes not only the possibility, but above all the requirement, of 'normality' for a diverse collective in which not all members wish to conform.

The right to marry and create a family has become the obligation to marry and create a family. It doesn't matter if you're not heterosexual, as long as you appear to be. It doesn't matter if you're a lesbian, but you must have children. Anyone practising a dissident sexuality is required to fit within the traditional family in all other aspects and reproduce the roles assigned to heterosexual couples.

The question 'Who's the woman?' or 'Who's the man?' is still common, as if a relationship in which everyone is themselves on equal terms cannot be imagined, not even when two people are of the same gender.

So, the idea of obligatory monogamy is added to obligatory heterosexuality, with a single relationship model possible. There's very little space for other options, such as group living in a commune or polyamorous alternatives, which have practically no representation in the media or any kind of legal recognition.

If a group of more than two people want to have a child, only two can have legal rights over it. If they want to marry, with all the rights this entails compared to being single, they cannot. The general understanding is that the social order is based on couples who will have children at some point, and although reality has led us to accept that monogamy is usually more feigned than actual, and usually more serial than eternal, we still refuse to accept that romantic love isn't the only way of loving.

Here we come back to how financial inequalities affect the freedom to live as we please: while for many years it's been accepted that men stay single and it's easier for them to have the financial resources at their disposal to be able to do so, women who can financially afford to be single continue to be suspected of some inadmissible defect if they don't have a partner.

In the same way, we can allow ourselves alternative ways of living to the extent that we don't depend on the community's support to survive. Polyamorous people who establish relationships with more than one person find it very difficult to 'come out of the closet', especially if they don't want to lose touch with family and those closest to them. Confessing to following a non-normative relationship model can often lead to losing a job or being expelled from certain circles.

The room of one's own, which represents the private space necessary for being a person in all their wholeness, isn't within everyone's reach. Presumably those who find it easiest to achieve are monogamous, financially independent heterosexual men. So, it should be no wonder to us that, starting from such unequal places, we then don't reach the same finish line.

Love Doesn't Kill

It's a familiar scene: someone appears and makes the rest of the universe disappear. All of a sudden, you only want to be with that person. You'd do anything for them. You love them more than anything else, you even love them more than yourself. The infatuation is mutual and the film conveniently ends when the characters are happy, almost always through a heterosexual frame and, in any case, invariably monogamous.

In our culture, there are some very clear rules stipulating what falling in love really is and how you must feel when it happens. I don't know how, against all evidence to the contrary, we've managed to build such a universal mythology of romantic love, and I find it even more surprising that, it being so oppressive, we find it so desirable.

There are four basic ideas about romantic love which we're force-fed through practically all artistic expression: true love is predestined, exclusive, all-powerful and the most important thing in life. When we say living without love isn't worthwhile, we don't mean love in general, we mean without falling in love with someone who feels the same way about us. The love for friends, family and even children (who are often seen as the fruit of a couple's love, not as people worthy of being loved in their own right) pales beside a story of romantic love.

Constructed ideas about how love should be are damaging because, to begin with, they generate unrealistic expectations about how a relationship should be and cause a lot of frustration, but, above all, because in many cases they impede the establishment of healthy relationships between equals. The model of love imposed on us pushes us to justify all too often behaviours we'd consider abusive in any other context. And, yes, women are the ones most in danger in this kind of relationship.

According to a 2023 UN report, more than five women or girls were killed every hour by someone in their own family in 2022, and 55 per cent of all female homicides are committed by intimate partners or other family members. Even so we continue believing and feeding the myths that reinforce this violence.

Even people of a certain age, who have fallen in and out of love a number of times, continue to believe that there is a better half – and only one – who will be our true love. This person, who will complement us and give us everything we lack, will be by our side all through life once we find the truly real thing.

'True love' is exclusive, there's only one right person and we must love only that person. Even though reality makes us anticipate the possibility of divorcing, when we break up with a partner it's because 'we made a mistake' and they weren't 'the one'.

However, the faithfulness requirement isn't symmetrical. Another very widespread myth is that women feel less sexual desire and only have sex if they're 'truly' in love. This discards any purely sexual affair outside the couple. In contrast, men are seen as beasts that don't know how to control their desires and, almost unwillingly, end up having sex with the first girl that goes by. If their partner finds out, they can easily claim that 'It meant nothing', but this argument is inconceivable if the woman is the unfaithful one. Since love can do anything, it can demand the wronged partner forgive the infidelity.

The fallacy that we can change for love and we're obliged to do so is especially frustrating. If you fall in love with someone, isn't it precisely for who they are? Why should you want them to change? And if someone loves you, will they require you to change your clothing or behaviour? Do they have the right to demand you don't see certain friends or stop doing things you like but they don't?

Women are required to give their all and be unselfish, and conflict is normalized, all in the name of love. According to a study from the Fundación Mujeres [Women's Foundation], 75 per cent of girls between 14 and 16, and 68 per cent of boys, think that it's acceptable for someone who loves you to mistreat you. We enter the world of coupledom assuming that the one who loves us will make us suffer, instead of thinking that someone who loves us should ensure the exact opposite. When the person we love abuses us, rather than being shocked, we think it natural. We even believe that if it's true love, it will endure anything.

Love is the most important thing of all, which is like saying that your partner is the most important thing of all. This often means cutting ties with the friends who could help us recognize the warning signs when abuse begins. We prioritize the relationship with our partner so much we stop doing activities of our choice, we give up our private spaces and we consent to our communication with others, the clothes we wear or how we behave in public being controlled. Our partner becomes the centre of our lives and we make everything else come second.

The manipulator in a toxic relationship demands the other's unconditional surrender because that's love, but it's not mutual. Controlling behaviour (if you love me, don't do this, don't dress like that, don't say such and such) is added to demands for exclusive attention and total availability (if you love me, come right now, don't meet your friends today). If the other person doesn't comply, they use emotional blackmail and martyrdom to get what they want (you've disappointed me, you've made me feel bad, I thought I could rely on you).

Certain behaviours which should set off women's alarm bells, like demanding their unconditional loyalty, seem not only natural but desirable. Many people think that the only abuse that can occur in a relationship is physical, but the first blow is the culmination of a process of isolation from those closest to them, gaslighting and destruction of the woman's self-esteem.

Manipulative women do exist, it's true, but there are two things that make them different from manipulative men: they rarely move on to physical abuse; and, while a man's worth is considered intrinsic, a woman's depends on the male gaze. We educate girls so their self-esteem totally depends on what men think of them, and this makes them fodder for abusers. We educate boys so they impose their view of things, and this facilitates their beginning to abuse without even being aware of it.

The traditional family structure, which relegates women to a room that isn't their own and for which they pay a very high price on a personal level, no doubt favours sexist violence too. There are some people that call it 'domestic', perhaps in an attempt to conceal that it's men killing women. Between 2003 and 2023, there were 1,237 'official' killings by (male) partners or ex-partners in Spain. The official figures don't include killings which have similar sexist motivations, but were committed by someone other than the victim's partner or ex-partner: for example, friends or family of the victim, or when prostitutes are killed by their clients.

Despite the worrying number of deaths, there is no terrorist alarm or urgent action plan for eradicating sexist violence. Citizens are more concerned about jihadists, even though the death toll from this kind of attack, in Spain for example, is seventeen over the last ten years and caused by the 2017 attacks in Barcelona and Cambrils. The sexist murders, like acknowledged terrorist killings, are motivated by an ideology – in this case, one that reinforces the idea not only that women are inferior to men and therefore abusing them is justified, but that they are property and can be controlled, instructed and expected to obey. The myth of romantic love contributes to normalizing this control.

The ideology of sexism, which few men will recognize so bluntly expressed, is strengthened by songs, sayings and all the paraphernalia of popular culture, and is expressed in many ways. From the most 'inoffensive' jokes about women in the kitchen, to mind-blowing comments like Trump's about the impunity of a rich man to treat women however he likes, to laws which deny women the right to make decisions about their own bodies, or high taxes on primary care products such as tampons: they are only the tip of an iceberg freezing all of society.

The ideological downpour that legitimizes men being more important than women because they earn more, do more prestigious work and receive more social recognition, at the same time shows them up as deficient beings who don't know how to take care of dirty clothes or of children, or of their own feelings. Women end up normalizing being at men's disposal to satisfy their emotional, familial, domestic and sexual needs . . . and men do too.

They feel justified in demanding; they find it natural. Just as their mother nurtured them when they were small, their wife will nurture them when they're grown. Social demands are very strict in this sense. Just as women who were educated with a promise of equality that they haven't seen fulfilled feel cheated, men educated to expect to have a slave happy to serve them also feel cheated when their partner demands they take their share of responsibility for housework or the children.

The difference is in the response: women usually accept the injustice or flee from it, and in contrast it's more likely that men will respond to situations they don't know how to handle with violence. In an experiment, a group of 8-year-old girls were placed in a room full of toy weapons; the impulse of many of the girls was to shoot themselves. The boys placed in the same set-up killed each other, but didn't pretend to injure themselves. As we've seen when discussing the machine gun fantasy, men have such a monopoly on violence that it doesn't even occur to many girls that they could kill someone else.

We definitely convince boys that it's normal to kill for love, and girls that it's normal to die for love. We need to banish phrases like 'love kills' from our way of speaking and start explaining that, if it kills, it isn't love – or it's a sick love that doesn't let us grow.

Substituting the fantasy of romantic love with a less damaging vision in which we relate to others as equals will be difficult. We're still a long way from believing that emotional relationships should enrich our lives, not impoverish them.

Men have an advantage over women when it comes to considering that there may be other priorities beyond being in a couple. The necessity of choosing between family (which is a couple plus children) and personal fulfilment in other areas (like work) is only raised for women. The dedication required from men and women in maintaining personal relationships is so unequal that men can have it all, but women must choose.

The women who choose to make something other than their partner or children the centre of their lives are judged harshly. Wouldn't a construction of love and relationships that bears the space for personal freedom more in mind be desirable? One that demands less unconditional giving and attains a more truly enriching exchange? Conditional love seems selfish, but it's much more reasonable. If you control me, you don't love me well; if you ridicule me, you don't love me well; if you're not excited by my successes, you don't love me well; if you don't treat me as an equal, you don't love me well.

The revolution in emotional relationships and proposals for new ways of loving is being led by feminists, and that's logical: women are the ones more likely to die in the attempt to turn the nightmare of romantic love, presented to them as the only legitimate dream, into reality.

Together We'll Take Back the Night

The streets belong to men. They stroll around in comfortable clothes, at any hour of the day, unconcerned by anything other than where they're going. Women try, but it's harder for them not to be reminded that their true place is at home.

Starting from urban planning, cities aren't thought out for people doing childrearing – a task traditionally considered to be for women – to have it easy. Moving around the city with a pushchair (let alone a wheelchair) is an almost impossible gymkhana of narrow pavements, ramp-less steps and Underground stations with no elevator.

Street lighting is known to play an important role in the rate both of robberies and of sexual assaults outside the home, but it isn't a priority and is less important than factors like saving money. Some say that light pollution is terrible and creates cities which are unsustainable. Don't we think the rate of rapes is terrible and unsustainable? How do we make a safe, and at the same time less polluting, city?

Signage in public spaces displays a person in trousers (which everyone sees as a man) to represent us all. When it displays a person in a skirt (which everyone sees as a woman), only women are represented – for example, next to toilets or seats reserved for mothers with children on public transport, which take for granted that in practice it will be the mothers and not the fathers taking care of children. It's true that this is how it is, by and large, but we can't lose the symbolic battle. If the little man in trousers represents us all, let him carry the kids.

Codes of etiquette and what clothing is appropriate or isn't are also completely sexist. Why shouldn't Western men wear skirts in the summer if it's more comfortable? Why can they bare their breasts if women can't?

But perhaps one of the clearest signs of male dominance of the streets are the behaviours we tolerate. Men catcalling women unknown to them is accepted as normal in our culture. Catcalls are nothing but unsolicited comments on the physical appearance of a woman who generally hasn't even looked at the man making the comment.

The general belief is that the woman should feel flattered, but the truth is there's no way of knowing how she'll feel. In fact, how she feels is irrelevant. The men who shout things at women on the street don't expect a response; they bank on the woman going on her way without saying anything, as occurs most of the time. If they were seeking interaction, it would be more effective to approach her respectfully and strike up a conversation, but to strike up a conversation she'd have to be considered worthy of talking to, which isn't the case.

It's a display of masculinity and dominance: I tell you what I think of your body because I'm very male and because I have the absolute right to. If they really wanted the woman to feel good when they catcall, perhaps they'd try to establish a less violent means of contact. I don't understand how shouting something usually unpleasant at someone who doesn't expect it is supposed to make them feel good. It's even more absurd when we consider that it's not really about the woman's physical appearance: we've all gone through it, however ugly or beautiful we are. We do know that wearing skirts or low-cut tops will mean comments, but wearing a tracksuit doesn't necessarily protect you from them.

When they're called out for their behaviour, men complain that they 'can't even look'. The truth is that we all look at the people we find attractive, but there's no need to be intrusive. You can look without making anyone uncomfortable and, above all, you can look and not say anything. The fact that the majority of women and men do it every day is proof.

It's true that 'catcalling' is less aggressive than touching someone's behind, but false that it's harmless. As soon as their breasts start to develop, girls are painfully aware that they're seen as pieces of flesh, with all that implies for self-esteem.

A few years ago, the hashtag #miprimeracoso [#myfirstharassment] appeared on Twitter, in which many women described the first time they felt harassed. Analysis of the 78,000 tweets using the hashtag shows that 40 per cent of the stories made reference to sexual assault and 60 per cent to verbal harassment in public spaces. The most startling piece of data is the average age at which this first harassment was suffered: 7 years old.

If having to face comments from strangers in public is unpleasant for an adult woman, it must be even worse for a young girl who still has no means of self-protection. The only way to cope is by becoming desensitized to it.

On the other hand, there's no way of knowing how far a stranger's catcall will go. Usually nothing happens, but the situation may become uncomfortable or even violent – and remember that, for the woman singled out by the catcall, the other person is a stranger. How do they know he won't follow or attack them? It's scary at night or in lonely places. Even if we keep in mind that some percentage of women must like being catcalled in public, this behaviour needs to be eradicated from public spaces, if only out of respect for those who suffer.

The freedom with which men give their opinion on a woman's appearance reminds women that they're not protagonists in their own lives, but a prop in men's. When they're in public, there's no respect for their personal space, no weighing up of the violence implied by them being forced to stop thinking about their own stuff to assess whether it's worth responding to the catcaller or better to move on as quickly as they can.

In her project 'El cazador cazado' [The Hunter Hunted], Alicia Murillo confronted the men who said things to her, recording them on her phone and asking them to repeat what they'd just said, to publish them later on the internet. The usual reactions deny the evidence: 'I didn't say anything to you'; try to undermine her self-esteem: 'you're so vain' or 'you're ugly'; invalidate whether she might consider it offensive or not, 'I didn't say anything offensive.' As a result of this project, she received an avalanche of insults and rape and death threats on social media.

The role reversal test, which usually serves to indicate whether a behaviour is sexist or not, doesn't work in this case. Many men say that they would love to be catcalled by women in public and therefore don't see doing this themselves as bad. However, they don't take into account that the situation is asymmetrical. On one hand, there's no possible comparison between the pressure about their bodies with the pressure about women's. On the other hand, as we've seen before, men's bodies aren't considered rapable and therefore fear doesn't come into it. The only way men understand the violence implied by catcalling or being touched in public spaces is if both the aggressor and the victim are men.

As a result of a campaign against harassment at the city festival in Tarragona, the man who was then editor-in-chief of the *Diari de Tarragona* newspaper (and whose name I won't say so as not to give him publicity) published an editorial in which, among many stupid things, he literally said: 'If a lady says no, it's maybe yes; if she says maybe, it's a yes; and if she says yes, she's not a lady.' Let's put this in context: it's the year 2016, in 21st-century Europe, and he's the editor-in-chief of a newspaper.

The massive backlash against this idiot led to his dismissal as editor of the paper, but he was retained as an 'adviser'. That is, he's been stripped of part of his symbolic power but continues to be paid.

The quote cited in the article totally eliminates a woman's agency in responding to men's propositions. It leaves no space for the negative, and opens the door to insistence when you've already said no and any person with a drop of sense would gracefully retire.

Among other pearls, the journalist also discusses 'seduction' and says that 'humanity would be wiped out' if men didn't insist. Maybe the pests would be wiped out, but certainly not humanity. Women would simply procreate with whom they want, not with those who force them.

Let's remember the context of the article: a campaign against sexual assaults at local festivals. The campaign doesn't interfere with people's sexual or loving games, it simply asks men not to abuse women.

Like everyone else, women don't need to be interpreted, they need to be listened to. Women usually show unmistakable signs of interest when they're interested. How come there are so many men who don't know how, or don't want, to read them?

Before approaching someone, trying to establish eye contact with them is recommended. If you've been looking at them for a while and they haven't looked at you even once, you needn't waste your time talking to them. It may also be that you consider yourself terribly interesting, you really saw something special in them and you want to know more. Responding in monosyllables is a clear indication that they have no interest in talking to you. People prefer to be friendly and answer questions put to them, but if they don't contribute to the conversation by asking other questions it usually means they don't feel like talking.

If you ask for their phone number and they say they don't have a mobile, there's no need to insist by asking for their email or to connect on social media. They certainly do have a mobile, but they don't want any further contact with you.

If they look at their phone or anywhere else while you're talking to them, it's a no. If they smile less and less, it's a no. If they tell you they have a partner, it's a no. If they say maybe some other time, it's a no. If they give you their number or Facebook because you've been pestering them but then don't answer messages or block you, it's a no. All this really is common sense, isn't it?

But if doubts still remain about when someone wants to have sexual relations with us and when they don't, there are various videos online about consent which use analogies to explain what is in no way consenting to sex. My favourite is the one comparing sex to a cup of tea.

When you offer a cup of tea, the other person can accept or refuse it. If they refuse, you don't need to make it, they've already told you they don't want it. If they accept it and you drink it together, fantastic. It might be frustrating if they accept a cup yet when you bring it over they don't feel like it, but throwing it over them isn't good. If they start to drink it but don't want to finish, they shouldn't be forced to. If they fall asleep or unconscious halfway through, we don't make them drink it with a funnel. Wanting to have tea with you one day doesn't mean that they'll always feel like it or that you can show up at their house with a thermos under your arm. And so on and so on.

All this may seem ridiculously obvious, but, remember, 80 per cent of rapes are committed by people who know the victim and they often say that the raped person consented. I think better education about what it means to give consent or not is worthwhile, but rejecting 'consensual' sexual relations altogether even more so. I don't want to have sex with someone who 'consents' to it, I want to have sex with someone who is dying to do it just as much as I am. If I make a sexual proposition and it's not enthusiastically accepted, maybe it's better to go for a walk or a coffee. Why do we assume that men must always want sex and women must 'give in' and that's that? Isn't it healthier to accept that men also have times when they don't feel like it, and that women should learn to be able to freely express their desire?

The idea that women 'are asking for it' when they're raped becomes even more perverse if we bear in mind that often they're not listened to when they say no.

Especially at night, the streets are unfriendly, but little by little we're taking them back. In *King Kong*

Theory, Virginie Despentes explains that she decided not to tell her parents when she was raped while hitch-hiking as an adolescent, because they would have wanted to shut her up at home and she didn't want to give up her freedom out of fear of assault. Yes, we may be attacked, and yes, we accept that it's the price we pay for moving around.

But we're not resigned to it: every day, there are more women taking self-defence classes or organizing to help one another. In the United States, Feminista Jones, an activist deeply involved in Black feminism, has driven the 'Are You Ok, Sis?' movement, which consists of offering help to women being pestered on the street with a very simple question: are you ok?

There are many advantages to this technique. It doesn't involve confronting the harasser, which makes it quite safe, but makes it clear that the other person isn't alone in the situation. Furthermore, it makes no assumptions about how the woman is feeling, simply offering her help. If we've been mistaken in assessing what's going on and it's a consensual situation, we won't have offended anyone. Finally, it creates a sense of complicity and companionship in surroundings that can be hostile.

It's no accident that a Black feminist came up with it: white women also suffer assaults, but there are even fewer consequences for assaulting a Black woman.

She's made even less of a person by the accumulation of discriminations by gender and by race.

I'd like to step aboard the boat of Feminista Jones, of Alicia Murillo, of all women who fight to seize the streets. Whether we are 20, or whether we are 40, may we take back the night together.

#Onsónlesdones

It was the start of summer and there was some political emergency – I don't remember which now. TV3 was broadcasting a special programme with seven experts, all men. Twitter began to boil over in the partial way social media does: since I follow many feminists, it seemed as though the programme was being criticized far and wide. They hadn't found a single woman capable of speaking accurately on the subject?

To us it seems normal to see only men in the media, because it's been this way all our lives. It seems so normal to us that it takes the feminist of the day to say: 'Hey, where are the women?' And then someone responds: 'It just happened, we were looking for an expert and this man came up.' Or 'He's a great journalist.' Or 'We can't hire someone just because they're a woman.' Or 'We tried to invite women, but they said no.'

Liz Castro thought that something needed to be done beyond spontaneous complaining and she sent a private message to a group of feminists on her Twitter timeline that she believed would be ready to step up. But what could we do? Another manifesto? We decided to be more ambitious: we organized ourselves to call out discrimination against women's opinions in the media in an insistent, systematic way online: #Onsónlesdones (#Wherearethewomen).

Numbering fifty people in no time, we created a blog, a Twitter account, a Facebook account, various working documents and even a logo. We also ended up deciding to draft a manifesto which attracted huge attention when it was launched and has almost 3,500 followers, as well as a list profiling experts to offer the media if they request it; the excuse for having no female experts can never be that there are none.

The idea is simple: count how many pundits there are in the media, separate them by gender and publish the result. At the start, the process seemed more complicated: how should we count them? The digital version of a newspaper or the paper one? Those classified by that same paper as 'op-eds' or any article stating an opinion? All this led us to the need for creating some clear criteria for counting – criteria which may not be perfect, but are fixed. The data shows what we already knew: there is a clear disparity.

Praise soon poured in, but so did criticism – the same as every time someone pushes for a more balanced representation of men and women in the media. The idea that we want to eject well-prepared men from the media to install mediocre women is as widespread as it is false. This assertion assumes that men are more worthy of giving opinion than women and the women installed would be mediocre.

This is disproved by the reality: there are a good number of mediocre men who could be substituted by talented people (men or women), because on top of sexism there are other forms of discrimination, such as class or racialization, not to mention having contacts within the media. If meritocracy were a perfect system, the representation of all kinds of people would be guaranteed, because there are talented people of all kinds.

Nor is it about ejecting anyone. All that's required is taking advantage of new hiring opportunities to include competent women until we reach a balanced system. Quotas aren't an end: they're a means to achieve a currently non-existent equality of opportunity. Obviously, there are men who are exceptional professionals, but there are also women who are exceptional professionals and we don't see them anywhere, or we don't see them to the degree reasonable to expect from looking at university students, for example, in degrees like journalism where there are

93

many more women than men (and this has been the case for long enough for some of them to already be experienced). On the other hand, we can't not hire someone because they are a woman, but there's no doubt that this is happening. There's no other explanation for such a huge bias in favour of men in the media, keeping in mind that there is a much more even distribution of talent in society.

Women already in the media sometimes fear being accused of being there 'by quota' and not for their value. It's a pity that only women wonder whether they have the right to be there or not (I've never heard anyone say 'He's there because he's a man', even though the system favours them regardless of their professional value). But it's also absurd reasoning. For example, journalists such as Empar Moliner or Mònica Planas put their name to the most widely read articles in *Ara* newspaper. It would be stupid to think that they would be there if they weren't competent.

The final argument of those in charge who do accept the need to balance the representation of men and women but can't see how to get there is that, often, when they invite certain women to participate, they refuse. This is true and there are multiple reasons. Lack of visibility is a fish that eats its own tail: since few are seen in the media, it seems few are capable of being there. We must make an effort to broaden our network of contacts, and trust databases such as the one maintained by the Institut Català de les Dones (Catalan Women's Institute), which offers a variety and quantity of qualified experts, but we must also put more pressure on those who select panelists. Things don't happen by chance and, if you look for an expert, men's names are easy to come by, because it's men who usually appear everywhere. But if 80 per cent of your panel of pundits are men and the first person that comes to mind to discuss a particular topic is a man, maybe you need to think a little longer, make a couple of calls, do a little research about which female experts there are in that field who might be good participants.

It's society that says no when women say they don't want to participate in the media. In general, the proposals they decline are badly paid or not paid at all. Women are already burdened with work inside and outside the home and this means there is less time to do anything that doesn't significantly contribute to work or the family, and personal fulfilment is expected to come later on, if there's a spare moment. Giving more advance notice to make organizing family matters possible would also favour the men who want to juggle things.

On the other hand, with regard to paid work in the public sphere, not only are we not advancing in equality, we're actually moving backwards. Economic crises strengthen backward-looking values in which the father of a family is the breadwinner: worrying for everyone, but even more so for the increasing number of families in which there is no father. Women receive less economic recompense because the assumption is that they have a husband to maintain them, but this is less and less the case. Therefore, they can't donate the time at their disposal to the media in the same way that well-known, well-paid men of a certain age can.

What's more, if there is a need to 'show your face', offer an opinion or display intelligence in the media, women have to fight against the generalized notion that men know more about it, are right more often and speak better. This idea goes against women who express an opinion in three ways: first, they're listened to with the preconception that they're surely mistaken (or they're not as right as the male panelist with whom they're debating); second, the belief affecting not only men but also women is that sometimes they prefer to stay quiet and listen.

Some women suffer so-called 'impostor syndrome' and question themselves to an unhealthy degree about whether they've prepared enough for certain requests, even though data shows that women study more and do more continuous training than men. This leads them to accept only the requests they can comfortably grasp, while most men have been socialized to be confident about their qualities. In this case, it's worth telling the professional women we want to hire how we value their experience and why their vision interests us. In this way, the topics of the talk can be more precisely defined, rather than keeping them general. This will also favour the men participating who are aware they can't know everything, so they could prepare better.

Finally, the third factor is that even women who feel certain of the validity of their opinions and arguments often prefer not to express them on broadcast media to avoid the personal critiques aimed at them, and being judged for non-professional reasons (whether they're well dressed or not, whether they're attractive or not, whether they're good mothers or not . . .). The media would do well to consider protocols of behaviour for attacks on social networks. The more protected they feel and the more support they have when facing insults, the safer women will feel in making their voices heard.

Obviously, all this shares 'the blame' for the disparity of representation in the media and explains the irregularity of the current situation, in which half the population seems excluded. And if 'the blame' is shared, so is the solution. Male media directors could dedicate more time and more effort to find female experts, journalists, pundits.

We could all come to realize that it's not normal (however usual it may be) to switch on the radio and hear four male voices for every one female, find eight photos of men in the paper for every one of a woman (and that one is an ad for perfume in which the woman is objectified, to boot). And when they are called and asked for their opinion, women could try to make a further effort and find the time and the courage to say 'yes', and the men they have by their side could try to make a further effort and find the time and the courage to cheer them on and make it easier for them (collecting children from school, making dinner, cleaning the toilet, reminding them that their opinion is worthwhile and it's good for it to be heard).

One of the successes of #Onsónlesdones is its perseverance when it comes to counting women and men in the media, but it was born to have a limited lifespan. All those who work at it would like to be able to hear, read and see people doing their work well in the most natural way. But in order to stop counting, a quick glance needs to be more encouraging than it is now.

After being counted for some years, the data confirms what can be seen at a glance: men are overrepresented in all op-eds in the media, except for television. The largest disparity is in print media, with the 80 per cent of male columnists unchanged in eight years of counting. The positive result from television, in contrast, is indeed a recent transformation: when the counting began, the participation of women was between 20 per cent and 40 per cent, depending on the programme. The good news is that a television programme where only men appear is beginning to be an outlier; the bad news is that the people who go on there are still white.

#Onsónlesdones has also begun to account for the appearance of racialized people and people of non-binary gender, and in both cases their presence is occasional. While the case of people of non-binary gender is understandable given the statistical rarity we still assume, in the case of racialized people there is no way to explain it other than structural racism. In the same way that showing only men doesn't reflect the make-up of society, neither does showing only white people. As the actress and anti-racism activist Yolanda Sey said at the 2024 Gaudí Awards gala, 'Catalonia is no longer only white', and it's time this was reflected in the media.

This disparity is universal: we find it among CEOs of communications companies, among programme directors, among talk-show guests . . . and, even more worryingly, in the view of gender they put forward.

As an example, we can look at a study in which Cambridge University analysed how athletes were discussed during the Rio Olympics in a database of thousands of articles. The adjectives used most often when discussing female athletes were 'big', 'pregnant', 'married', 'single', while those for male athletes were 'fast', 'strong', 'incredible' and 'fantastic'. As in every other sphere, the women were judged by their age and their relationship with men (whether they were married or had children). In contrast, men were judged by their qualities.

The media reinforce stereotypes to the point of satiety. Stereotypes aren't bad because they're false, they're bad because they cancel out any other possible reality. It's not that women weaker than men don't exist – and they possibly make up the majority – but if they're the only ones we see we can reach the conclusion that there are no other kinds. The media must make an effort to show the much more varied reality and discuss everything in a less sexist way.

Meanwhile, the images shown of women are hypersexualized. In the case of athletes that we examined, many photographs show them in regulation uniforms which require them to show much more skin than their male colleagues competing in the same sport. Likewise, athletes who remain covered from head to toe because of their country of origin's cultural imperatives are criticized. We must conclude that the imposition of how much flesh women are obliged to show or cover up is what unites all cultures.

By default, sport is male, which we call simply 'sport': if men don't participate, it's called 'women's sport'. The many programmes dedicated to male football don't clarify that they'll only talk about men; it's taken for granted. As in all fields, there are disparities in salaries, resources, attention … Men do universal things, women do women's things.

But leaving this obvious reality to one side and returning to #Onsónlesdones, the group's way of working interests me more than the objective. There's no hierarchy: someone makes a suggestion and the rest give their opinion. If it's approved, someone takes responsibility for pushing it forward. We have no fixed representatives and respond to demands for participation in the media, discussions and round tables (of which there are many) according to the availability and interests of each person. Nothing is demanded of anyone: everyone does what they can or want to. The most interesting thing is that this anarchic leaderless mechanism works perfectly.

One curious piece of data: since the creation of the collective, some men (a few) have offered to help us, often telling us how they believe we could be more effective. That is, even our allies come to school us, as if having had the idea, driving the group forward, and doing the daily work aren't sufficient credentials to show that we know what we're doing. When we've invited them to participate by collaborating with the count, the heaviest workload and one we need to take turns at, not a single one has been interested. On the other hand, we've found many male collaborators in spreading the group's objectives, its manifesto and monthly reports. Some have even adopted the struggle as their own and joined us in demanding more equitable representation from those in charge of the media.

The School of Life

School is one of the most important elements of socialization because it's where the shared values agreed on by society are expressed. Families may promote a very broad and, in some cases, opposing range of values, but the school – especially a state school – transmits the values we share. Nevertheless, school isn't a homogeneous thing and is made up of people who also have their own value systems, which doesn't always coincide with the values the school should promote.

Despite the efforts of many female teachers (we'll use the word 'female' because they make up an indisputable majority) to introduce co-education in schoolrooms, and the rule in Spain that classes in public schools should be mixed, not only is equality not promoted by example, but also the usual discriminations in all other aspects of society are actually reproduced. Maybe we believe that as people we deserve the same rights sufficiently to enshrine them in law, but don't agree that we deserve the same opportunities in practice. If we did believe it a little more, inequality wouldn't be so widespread in the educational system, the default loudspeaker of social values.

Firstly, the curriculum is totally androcentric. The thinkers, writers and history-makers studied are always male. It is said that there haven't been as many important women as men in history and here we go again, same as ever: what is important and what isn't are judged according to what pertains to men and is considered universal. Without the tasks tradition-ally undertaken by women, like childrearing and the maintenance of social cohesion, there'd be no history to speak of. However, I'll not find anything in text-books about how childrearing was organized in the sixteenth century, but I'll get endless lecturing about the Corts [the Catalan Courts].

At the same time, the women who did do 'impor-tant things', according to androcentric values, are silenced. Why do we in Catalonia study the misogy-nist Jaume Roig and not the proto-feminist Isabel de Villena, contemporaries of the fifteenth century? In its time, *Vita Christi* was more widely read than *Tirant lo Blanc*. It's discussed within feminist studies, but not in literary studies where it also belongs.

In the sixteenth century, during the Council of Trent when authors who interpreted the sacred scriptures like Villena were censured, she was silenced. It's taken five centuries to reclaim her, but she hasn't reached the curriculum. To read her, you have to scratch beneath officialdom.

Women who achieve 'important' feats are systematically erased: the female painters who worked in Renaissance studios are hidden, and Nobel Prizes which wouldn't have been possible without the team's female scientists are attributed to men. Rosalind Franklin was instrumental in the discovery of the structure of DNA, but the Nobel was carried off by three men: Francis Crick, James Watson and Maurice Wilkins. Even though Rosalind was already dead and couldn't have won it, she wasn't even mentioned.

Anthony Hewish won the Nobel Prize for Physics in 1974 for a discovery that had actually been made by his pupil Jocelyn Bell Burnell. The grounds for not including her in the prize are that the intellectual property of discoveries made by pupils belongs to their tutors, however little they are involved in the research. Truly, this seems like a flimsy excuse.

From an early age, we learn that men are the ones who do important work and women are at home cooking and looking after someone, which are not important tasks and have little prestige. The assumption is that paid work of any kind is more important than the unpaid caring work done mostly by women.

If you're a boy, how do you not look down on those who don't contribute to society in a meaningful way? If you're a girl, how do you not doubt your own abilities? This paradigm leads to two evils. There is the previously mentioned impostor syndrome: women mistrust their own abilities to an unreasonable degree, when they have higher levels of education, get better marks and do more continuous training in adult life than men. In contrast, men have excessive confidence that isn't always justified: they don't doubt their ability even when it would be reasonable to do so, and this leads to great frustration after small failures. When failure is the only option, it's hard to throw yourself in the pool, but when failure isn't even imagined, you could throw yourself in the pool when there isn't enough water.

Meanwhile, boys are pushed to study sciences and girls literature, in tandem with the humanities' loss of prestige: if you must study something, make it something unimportant. Medicine is one of the few science degrees in which there are more girls than boys and it is suspiciously linked to caring.

Prejudices about abilities differing by gender are just that – prejudices. Computer science is a clear example: the women who did the boring calculations by hand now done by machines were called computers. By the time personal computers came out during the 1980s, they were marketed as a product that could broaden work horizons for boys; marketing departments didn't bank on families spending so much money on a toy for girls.

This gender bias has resulted in an imbalance in students of computer science from the 1990s onwards, whereas an equal number of men and women studied it before the eruption of advertising.

The subjects are androcentric and so are the prejudices about individual abilities, but the discrimination doesn't end there: boys are the speakers par excellence in class. Studies show not only that boys raise their hands more, but also that it's much more likely they'll be permitted to speak when they do so without raising their hands. In contrast, girls are called to order when they speak out of turn.

The widespread idea that women speak much more than men is totally false in mixed groups. Studies show that men enjoy more turns to speak than women, and for longer. They also interrupt others more, especially if they're women.

From an early age, girls are trained to self-regulate: they're socially sanctioned for being assertive and must think much more about not only what they say, but how they say it. Generally, women are listened to less and it's taken for granted that they don't know what they're talking about. I suggest an experiment.

Drum up a person of the opposite sex. In a mixed conversation, have the woman express an idea. Five minutes later, the man will repeat it and appropriate it for himself. If someone tells him, 'She already said that a while ago', you can party: you've come across a group where someone had their ears open to systematic discrimination.

In an article, the author Soraya Schemaly suggested teaching girls three phrases:

I already said that.
Don't interrupt me.
No need to explain it to me.

The first is specifically to avoid women being ignored when they speak and men appropriating their ideas. The second is to break male dominance over turns to speak. The third is to avoid so-called mansplaining, in which a man who probably knows less than his conversationalist about the subject explains what she's just said back to her. The message is clear: they must be pretty and submissive, not clever and challenging. A good girl is a quiet, still, almost dead but smiling girl, as shown in all advertising.

Female teachers must pay more attention to these seemingly unimportant details, which contribute to reinforcing the confidence of some (boys) and the lack of confidence of others (girls). This will help girls to be more self-confident when expressing their opinions and help boys to see their female colleagues as equals and not simpletons with few opinions.

As well as the sexism of the curriculum imposed by the establishment and the sexist behaviour tolerated or even promoted by certain teachers, the sexism practised by the pupils themselves – increasingly intense, the older they get – must be included.

If many of the social rules ascribing different roles to us depending on gender aren't internalized during nursery school, they're powerfully reproduced in primary school and mercilessly in secondary. Bullying, the most violent form of discrimination at school, is based on social rules concerning how our physical appearance should be, but also on racist and sexist prejudices.

If the teaching staff hear and tolerate very common comments like 'Shut up, gayboy', or 'What a slut, she's done it with half the school', in the yard if not in the classrooms, they're implicitly supporting these statements and also missing an opportunity to educate about the right to be respected.

The emotional and sexual volatility typical of adolescence can be added on top of bullying in secondary schools. All the sexism within couples we've discussed is repeated in first relationships, with the additional danger that idealization of romantic love is even stronger during adolescence than in adulthood. Lack of experience puts boys in the position of having to reproduce the hegemonic role of the dominant male, and leaves girls without the resources to demand more healthy relationships. If the model at home isn't positive and egalitarian, we're lost: the ruling myths about romantic love are difficult to avoid and peer pressure will force compliance with its requirements.

Certain controlling situations are so normalized for us that the group not only fails to detect abuse, but actually celebrates it. When a boy boasts to his friends that he has 'persuaded' his partner to have sex with him, even though she wasn't very sure, pressuring her to exhaustion, his friends congratulate him instead of stopping him in his tracks and making him see that no one should be coerced.

The ideological abyss between girls and boys continues to grow. While a large number of younger girls have taken on the most basic principles of feminism, sexist ideas aren't only still in fashion among their male peers, they are being radicalized by them. The *Público* newspaper has analysed data from CIS [Centro de Investigaciones Sociólogicos: Center for Sociological Investigation] from 1987 to 2023 and found that young boys are positioning themselves further and further to the right and embracing traditionalist ideologies about every person's place in the world, while girls are veering to more left-wing positions. It remains to be seen where the ideological battle will be decided in future elections, in a political context where the centre is increasingly shifting to the right.

Luckily, there are enlightened teachers in many schools, lessons reflecting on gender violence are being given and the most flagrant types of discriminations have been eliminated. But we can't forget that co-education isn't only bringing boys and girls together in a classroom, but also giving them the same opportunities to develop their personal abilities and offering them a safe and respectful environment.

This is where we are failing our young people.

We Don't Want to Wear the Trousers

However foolish it may seem, given the state in which politicians, businessmen and powerful men in general have left the world up to now, feminists don't want to kick men out of politics. There's no proof that women could necessarily do better, even though the truth is that it would be difficult to do worse. Feminist demands are more about having political representatives not only on the register, but also at the highest echelons of decision-making. And that traditionally male values needn't be adopted to be able to get there.

There's no need to reiterate the over-representation of men – it's obvious that they occupy all relevant roles, but let's take a look at the most symbolic one in Catalonia. Female presidents of the Generalitat de Catalunya (Catalonia's autonomous government) in the entire history of the institution: zero. Female presidents of Spain in the entire history of the institution: zero.

At the age of 6, the aspirations of boys and girls are similar. They want to be lots of different things, but there's no separation of aspiration by gender. At 12, boys say they want to be president of the country, doctors, footballers. Girls: teachers, nurses, actresses. It's not that they no longer want to be president, but they know they won't be able to. It takes them six years to learn their place in society and have 'realistic' aspirations.

Despite Spain's 'zipper system' which imposes on lists of candidates a certain parity by law (of every five people, there must be two or three of each gender), such lists are usually headed by men. A very thorough study was done in Baix Llobregat in Catalonia: 46 per cent of the candidates on the ballot were female, as required by law, but they topped only 25 per cent of the lists. The message is 'Come be part of the gang since it's obligatory, but you're not going to be mayor.'

In recent years, equal representation has advanced spectacularly: according to a study by economist Carme Poveda, in 2023 the government of Catalonia was close to reaching total parity, with some 49 per cent of positions of responsibility being held by women. Despite the positive picture overall, if we look at the detail we can see that the majority of these positions are clustered in Equality, Social Rights, Culture, Foreign Action and Health, while Economy, Climate, Universities, Territory and Internal Affairs continue to be led by men.

Some parties allege that their base doesn't have an equal number of women and men participants: there are many more men than women and it's normal that more of them rise through the ranks. Among the many possible explanations, let's remember that family needs are asymmetrical: men aren't asked how they juggle political life and family life, only women are questioned in this way.

Men can invest the 7 additional hours of house-work women do compared to men into participating in political life, leaving their partners to take on their share of domestic obligations.

On the other hand, you have to be very self-assured to expose yourself to the brutal criticism received by women in politics, which is often personal and not about their role or their work.

Some members of the CUP (Popular Unity Candidacy) reached the point of reading a manifesto in response to the insults they received: their bodies, their physical appearance, the number of their sexual partners were all criticized; their political worth, not once.

As always, some allege that male politicians are also criticized for their appearance. It's not the same at all: criticisms of male politicians aren't made while supported by a social structure putting maximum pressure on women to be attractive, and there's no suggestion that the only personal value that they can bring to society is their physique.

A joke made about the then-president of the Government of Catalonia Artur Mas on the TV show *Polònia*, in which he called himself 'handsome' and thanked himself for the compliment, did indeed discuss his physique. However, the criticism wasn't about whether he was handsome or ugly, but his vanity. Besides, vanity in men can be considered self-confidence, and therefore a positive characteristic in politics.

This exposure to the harshest criticisms (which might include threats of rape, not usually made to men) not necessarily related to work may contribute to many thinking very carefully before opening themselves to it.

Those who risk and achieve a visible position still suffer double discrimination: to get there they have to 'be like a man' but 'look like a woman'.

When women in politics are discussed, the most frequent models (because there aren't that many to choose from) are Margaret Thatcher and Angela Merkel, who uphold the traditionally masculine qualities associated with leadership: inflexibility, firmness, assertiveness. And for precisely this, they are criticized: what is considered positive in a male politician, in a female politician is considered aggressive. Allegedly, they didn't bring any supposedly feminine qualities to politics – but on the other hand anyone trying to is blocked.

Margaret Thatcher took classes with a speech therapist who taught her to use a deeper voice and speak in a more assertive manner, with fewer speech modifiers. Women say 'in my opinion', 'it seems to me that', 'I would say', 'I think', 'maybe' much more often, and seek confirmation from those listening more frequently. It's not always that women feel unsure, but when they speak with confidence and make it clear that they know what they're talking about it's very easy for them to be accused of being arrogant. Thatcher's advisers knew that these speech markers made her seem 'soft' and she had to be the Iron Lady.

Many more women come to power in an 'interim' manner, at an exceptional time, not during the normal course of elections. The Danish series *Borgen* is an interesting reflection of this: it analyses the public and private lives of a woman who inadvertently finds herself prime minister. Women are the Plan B set in motion when everything has gone wrong, as during the Second World War: with the majority of men at the front, it was necessary to resort to women's hands so that the factory production needed to carry on the war didn't stop.

Every time it seems that the system is collapsing and we don't know how to get out of a crisis making the gap between rich and poor ever more abysmal, the debate about whether a more 'female' leadership would achieve more cooperative, democratic, peaceful political practices arises.

But what are we referring to when we talk about female leadership? Learned femininity is about submission, denial of the self and the idea that others (sons, male companions, male friends and men in general) are more important than you. Perhaps because of this, women are more ready to argue with the aim of reaching an agreement and not of imposing their vision or winning the argument.

Women are born losers – or, rather, have been inconsiderately socialized to get used to losing, in such a way that reaching an agreement already seems like a victory. If the two sides of a negotiation are represented by women and they reach agreement, both will feel that they've won something. This is fantastic if we want to be truly cooperative and democratic, but unfortunately it's not usually so.

Beyond representation, if we examine the policies for equality that have been implemented, they are merely decorative. They're not discussed in electoral debates and seem optional. The Spanish Law for Equality of Men and Women of July 2015 remains as unfulfilled by parties as it was unanimous when they passed it.

Besides, the text is packed with expressions like 'should tend to include', 'must try', 'must drive', which make it very easy not to advance at all. 'Tend to include' isn't 'include', 'try' isn't 'demand', 'drive' isn't 'change'. It's a law written not to be complied with but to feign that something is being done.

Even though sexism affects 100 per cent of the population and prevents 51 per cent having the same opportunities as the privileged 49 per cent – not earning the same salary or enjoying the same respect – the policies aiming to guarantee equality for all citizens are considered 'complementary' to the 'important' issues, which are resolved from a male perspective.

A more intersectional vision is required. Equality cannot be a bastion of annoying feminists who need to be kept happy so they don't make too much noise: it must cover everything. Feminism is the only revolution which has the equality of rights and practical opportunities for all of humanity as its objective; we can't allow it to be considered a secondary matter.

The androcentric vision so deeply shapes the actions of administrations that many people's lives can actually be endangered. Although, thanks to the feminist and anti-racism struggle from the 1980s onwards, illnesses that didn't affect only white men began to be studied, and advances like the recognition and communication of symptoms of serious health problems that differ between the sexes – for example, heart attacks – were achieved, much remains to be done. Illnesses that mostly affect women, such as fibromyalgia or endometriosis, continue to attract less research than those affecting men. The development of the male contraceptive pill has halted several times because of the side effects it might have for the men taking it, which on close examination are far less severe than those of the contraceptive pill women have been taking for decades.

Luckily, our grandmothers' fight has had some effect and feminism has achieved some of its goals. The majority of Europeans believe that women should have equal rights and opportunities (there are even some who think they've been achieved). They might even come to believe that it's also women's turn to be in charge a while, for a change.

But girls have learned that the jobs to which they can aspire are the ones related to caring for others, and boys have learned to assert themselves. They have every reason to think the world belongs to them: the politicians, the entrepreneurs, the rich and powerful are generally men. We see them on the news, we read them in newspapers, they govern our lives.

There is a dark side to the socialization of a winner, though: why should they respect rules? They're men.

Why should they accept being told 'no'? The most radical not only become frustrated when they're not listened to, some take action as a consequence. Let's recall once more the over-representation of men among violent criminals.

Clearly, we must begin to educate boys as we're educating girls. Feminizing not only politics but society as a whole is urgently needed. All people must learn to respect others as girls are taught to.

The longer we don't do this, the more any measure we might take will be just a patch that doesn't fix the underlying problems. A more feminine way of doing politics doesn't mean politics only exercised by women, but instead by people who recognize how harmful the values of traditional masculinity are for society. If we want more just policies, we shouldn't want women to wear the trousers, we should want everyone in charge to wear skirts, if I may be permitted so simple a metaphor.

Being Nothing to Be Everything

It's a boy. It's a girl.

It's like being condemned to life imprisonment with a pink uniform, with a blue uniform. The sentence is pronounced with the list of rules and we're pinched every time we break them, until we're tamed.

If we're lucky, we'll find things we like on the list. If not, we'll have to learn to pretend. But what happens when we can't pretend any more?

When I was born, they said I'd be a woman. For forty years I lived it, tried it out, thinking the problem wasn't being a woman per se, but being unable to adjust to what I was permitted and what I wasn't as a woman. I tried to expand the box, make the list of things I liked doing as a woman longer. For a long time, I played the role asked of me on the required occasions. If necessary, I could pretend I was a 'normal' woman. Looking at photos of me at 30, I could pass for a heterosexual, monogamous mother of a family, however absurd that seems if you look at me now. When I walked down the street, people must have only seen a woman, and everything else could be invented. A husband and children, maybe a job. They could imagine me as submissive and quiet, happy to shave, reading fashion magazines.

When I'd get home and close the door, I could stop pretending because, little by little, as we grow older, we recognize each other, those of us who don't quite fit in. We lose the fear of silence and those who would also like to speak come closer. Suddenly, we don't know how, we're surrounded by other people pretending a lot of the time.

More and more, we stop pretending. We party where it's not necessary, where no one expects us to act in any particular way. We have partners and friends that aren't frightened off by us being as we are; we read books by other dissidents; we organize among ourselves.

When we feel there's enough of us, we start shouting. We go to Pride parades or demand rights for trans people. We hold conferences about intersexuality, we tell each other about the oddities we share. The day comes when we pretend only very occasionally. When we move around alone at night – or at work, if necessary.

But what happens to the people who can't pretend? My trans girlfriends who know that there are places even more dangerous for them than for me. The person who doesn't feel themself to be a man or a woman and dresses without following any rules. They're always looked at twice, they're a question made flesh. Sometimes they're shouted at. Sometimes they're followed. Sometimes they're stripped in an attempt to dispel doubt, as if the essence of what we are can be found in our genitals.

All these comrades with dissident bodies and expressions are perhaps what most helps me advance in feminism. Their fight to be who they are makes space for me to be who I am. Their untying the corset helps me breathe a little easier. Their consideration of the limits of gender pushes me to consider my own, to the point that I've finally given in. I don't believe in it, this division between men and women. To me it seems a cheap (but very expensive for us) excuse to exert power and violence. I don't see how having the potential ability (and under no circumstances the obligation) to gestate and give birth justifies the burden of gender, which spews so many absurd rules on us. I refuse. I won't participate. I declare myself out of the box. I declare myself out of the game. I commit to actively destroying the mirage of binarism.

This doesn't mean ignoring the fact that the world doesn't yet work this way, and that we people who have decided to stray from the norm are so denied our place that society pretends we don't exist. As if denying us words will make us disappear, as if denying us language can prevent us from saying that we're here, happy to resist, even bloom, among so much shit.

I've tried to explain how the world is, everything it does wrong, everything that needs to change. But I'd like to end by imagining a very free space. A not too distant future that, if I don't live to see it, my little ones will. A place where it isn't necessary to be anything, and where you can be everything you are. A corner of the world inhabited by people who live with people, admire people, respect people. That world I was told when I was growing up might exist, and where I wouldn't have to pretend anything – just be me.

Feminist Mini-lexicon:
25 Words for Naming Reality

Agency: the capacity of people to act in an autonomous way, with their own criteria and subordinate to no one.

Agender: a person who doesn't identify with any gender.

Asexual: a person who feels no sexual attraction, or who feels little or no desire to have shared sexual relations.

Cisgender (cis): a person who identifies with the gender assigned to them at birth.

Cissexism: systemic prejudice in favour of cis people.

Compulsory heterosexuality: the assumption that all people are heterosexual.

Cultural appropriation: exploitation of the culture of a marginalized group by members of a dominant or privileged group, normally without understanding its history, experiences or traditions (for example, a white person wearing traditional Chinese dress).

Gender binary / gender binarism: system which only recognizes 'man' and 'woman' as possible genders and therefore marginalizes anyone who doesn't identify as such.

Gender expression: outward manifestation of gender identity through clothes, hairstyle, etc. Gender expression (independent of gender identity) is the main element that society takes into account to assign you to the women group or the men group. A person with a normative gender expression (for example, a cis man who wears his hair short, wears trousers and dark-coloured clothing) is less likely to suffer discrimination in public (spaces) than a person with a non-normative gender expression (for example, a man who wears his hair long, make-up or skirts). Gender expression doesn't necessarily indicate gender identity, and sexual orientation even less so.

Heteronormativity: the belief that heterosexuality is the only natural, normal expression of sexuality.

Internalized misogyny: involuntary assumption of the sexist messaging present in society or culture. Internalized misogyny influences women to reinforce sexism.

Intersexuality: refers to a combination of hormones, anatomical features and chromosomes which fall outside the norm. The gender is assigned according to anatomy at birth. In the event that doctors can't unambiguously sex the child, the karyotype and hormonal system can be analysed. The legal imperative for registering newborns as male or female, with no other options, means that there is no recognition of the existence of intersex people. Often they are mutilated or given hormonal treatments to better fit into one of the two groups, without bearing their health or right to bodily integrity in mind.

Male chauvinist pig: a man, usually cis and straight, who feels comfortable being sexist and has no intention of changing.

Male gaze: presentation of the male perspective as the only valid and existing one in the media, in advertising, in fiction, etc.

Mansplainer: a male chauvinist pig of a certain age and social position who pontificates with an absolute lack of awareness, often in the media.

Misandry: don't worry, it doesn't exist.

Misogyny: hatred for women.

Pansexual: a person who feels attracted to people of all genders.

Patriarchy: social organization marked by the supremacy of the father in the clan or family. In truth, the control by men of a disproportionate amount of power (as 49 per cent of the population, men control 99 per cent of resources).

Privilege: combination of advantages (or lack of sanctions) which a majority group enjoys.

Queer: a person who doesn't identify as cisgender and/or heterosexual.

Rape culture: normalization of violence through social attitudes towards gender, sex and sexuality.

Sexual orientation: the attraction (physical, emotional, romantic, aesthetic or any other kind of attraction) that a person feels for others.

Toxic masculinity: socially constructed attitudes which require men to be violent, emotionless, sexually aggressive, etc.

Transgender (trans): a person who doesn't identify with the gender assigned to them at birth.

Sources

Scientific articles and in-depth studies from which the cited data came (however incredible it may seem, I didn't make up a single stat!):

Cestero Mancera, Ana María (2007). 'Cooperación en la conversación: estrategias estructurales características de las mujeres'. *Linred: Lingüística en la Red*, 5, Universidad de Alcalá. Available at: http://hdl.handle.net/10017/24466.

Enguix, B. (2012). 'Cultivando cuerpos, modelando masculinidades'. *Revista de Dialectología y Tradiciones Populares*, 67.

Esteban Galarza, M. L. (2004). *Antropología del cuerpo: género, itinerarios corporales, identidad y cambio*. Ediciones Bellaterra.

Franzoi, S. L. & Shields, S. A. (2010). 'The Body Esteem Scale: Multi-dimensional Structure and Sex Differences in a College Population'. *Journal of Personality Assessment*, 48.

Gómez Granell, Carme & Marí-Klose, Pau (2012). *Infància, Adolescència i Família: un anàlisi del Panell de Famílies i Infància*. CIIMU. Available at: http://institut infancia.cat/wp-content/uploads/2016/02/2012-IV-informe-Estudi-cat-1.pdf.

LoBue, V. & DeLoache, J. S. (2011). 'Pretty in Pink: The Early Development of Gender-Stereotyped Colour Preferences'. *British Journal of Developmental Psychology*, 29(3), 656–67. Available at: https://doi.org/10.1111/j.2044-835X.2011.02027.x.

Patterson, M. M. & Bigler, R. S. (2006). 'Preschool Children's Attention to Environmental Messages about Groups: Social Categorization and the Origins of Intergroup Bias'. *Child Development*, 77(4), 847–60. Available at: https://doi.org/10.1111/j.1467-8624.2006.00906.x.

Puntoni, S., Sweldens, S. & Tavassoli, N. T. (2011). 'Gender Identity Salience and Perceived Vulnerability to Breast Cancer'. *Journal of Marketing Research*, 48(3), 413–24. Available at: https://doi.org/10.1509/jmkr.48.3.413.

Smith, C. & Lloyd, B. (1978). 'Maternal Behaviour and the Perceived Sex of Infant: Revisited'. *Child Development*, 49(4), 1263–6. Available at: https://doi.org/10.2307/1128775.

Soleto Ávila, Marisa (ed.) (2014). 'Coeducación y mitos del amor romántico'. *Revista Mujeres*, monográfico info 93. Available at: www.fundacionmujeres.es/attachments/show/364_BOLETIN%20FM%2093.pdf.

Wanless, S. B., McClelland, M. M., Lan, X., Son, S.-H., Cameron, C. E., Morrison, F. J. & Sung, M.

(2013). 'Gender Differences in Behavioral Regulation in Four Societies: The United States, Taiwan, South Korea, and China'. *Early Childhood Research Quarterly*, 28(3), 621–33. Available at: https://doi.org/10.1016/j.ecresq.2013.04.002.

Websites consulted

https://ec.europa.eu/eurostat/statistics-explained/index
.php?title=Crime_statistics.
https://violenciagenero.igualdad.gob.es/violenciaEnCifras
/victimasMortales/fichaMujeres/2023/VMortales_2023
_11_08.pdf.
https://premsa.cambrabcn.org/wp-content/uploads/2023
/11/Estudi-Generalitat_sector-public_PPT_2023_in
formecomplet_ODEE-1.pdf.
www.unwomen.org/en/digital-library/publications/2023
/11/gender-related-killings-of-women-and-girls-
femicide-feminicide-global-estimates-2022.